Enjoy the path to healthy
eating...

Also by Michael Psilakis

How to Roast a Lamb

LIVE TO EAT

Cooking the Mediterranean Way

MICHAEL PSILAKIS

with

Kathleen Hackett

PHOTOGRAPHY AND DESIGN
Hirsheimer & Hamilton

LITTLE, BROWN AND COMPANY
NEW YORK BOSTON LONDON

Little, Brown and Company
Hachette Book Group
1290 Avenue of the Americas, New York, NY 10104
littlebrown.com

First Edition: January 2017

Little, Brown and Company is a division of Hachette Book Group, Inc. The Little, Brown name and logo are trademarks of Hachette Book Group, Inc.

The publisher is not responsible for websites (or their content) that are not owned by the publisher.

The Hachette Speakers Bureau provides a wide range of authors for speaking events. To find out more, go to hachettespeakersbureau.com or call (866) 376-6591.

ISBN 978-0-316-8013-3
LCCN 2016934518

10 9 8 7 6 5 4 3 2 1

IM

Printed in Singapore

To my wife, Anna, who somehow finds the strength to endure the chaos of restaurant life, all the while ingeniously finding ways to maintain some sense of normalcy. Your strength is why our family is.

To my son Gabriel, our first born, our cherub, who sees good in all and has a heart filled with compassion, joy, and love. The world would be a better place if everyone saw it through your eyes.

To my son Zachary, my rebellious twin, your strong convictions, resolve, and inner strength will open a path that you will one day undoubtedly lead, but your guarded inner voice will help you choose right from wrong.

CONTENTS

RECItPE INDEX

FISH

FOREWORD
Tassos C. Kyriakides, PhD

EATING THE MEDITERRANEAN WAY IS ONE OF THE SUREST PATHS WE HAVE toward greater health. Through many years of research, the medical and scientific communities have established that Mediterranean nutrition can prevent or significantly reduce the risk of coronary heart disease, stroke, and type 2 diabetes, and can be an effective way to maintain a healthy weight.

A true Mediterranean plate elegantly blends the richness of seafood, the simplicity of greens, vegetables, and legumes, and the power of extra virgin olive oil. Meats and carbohydrates appear rarely, but no severe restrictions are imposed. This healthy way of eating is appealing and sustainable because it does not sacrifice pleasure or convenience for health.

This is why it is a joy to join chef Michael Psilakis in the kitchen. His recipes invigorate the food of the Mediterranean with new flavor, and his method of building dishes from seven essential staples makes it easier than ever to cook and eat the Mediterranean way at home.

As you embark on the flavorful ride that is *Live to Eat*, take note of these ingredients: olive oil, Greek yogurt and feta cheese, and garlic.

OLIVE OIL

Beyond the historical, cultural, and emotional connection that people in the Mediterranean region have to the olive and its oil, their health has been positively affected through its abundant consumption. Many of these benefits stem from monounsaturated fatty acids, which have been shown to reduce the risk of heart disease and to lower total and low-density lipoprotein cholesterol levels. Recent evidence suggests that cardiovascular disease shares common mechanisms with emotional health as it relates to nutrition; conditions such as depression may benefit from the fatty acids found in olive oil. Oleocanthal, another nutrient in olive oil, counters inflammation and is a protective agent against breast cancer. Increased consumption of olive oil is also associated with a reduced risk of skin cancer.

GREEK YOGURT AND FETA

Both feta cheese and Greek yogurt are cultured milk products, which are beneficial to gut health. Cultured milk helps colonize the digestive system with healthy microorganisms that protect the gut flora from organisms that can cause infections. The process of culturing can restore digestive enzymes that help the body absorb calcium and other minerals and elevate levels of vitamins B and C. This process is beneficial for bone health as it can slow down bone deterioration and loss. Regular use of cultured dairy products can also help lower cholesterol. However, it should be noted that feta can be high in cholesterol and sodium, so its use should be moderated. Its common presentation in the form of small crumbs helps to strike that balance.

GARLIC

Throughout history, garlic has been used for culinary as well as medicinal purposes, primarily as a supplement to increase vitality. The body of modern scientific evidence has primarily focused on the benefits that garlic imparts to cardiovascular health by helping reduce blood pressure and cholesterol, and by reducing the risk of hardening of arteries. Garlic has also been shown to assist in lowering the risk of gastrointestinal cancers as well as boosting immune system function.

As you cook and eat these dishes, you will be mesmerized by scent and flavor, and pleased by all the other benefits of this healthy triad. As the title of this book suggests, we should strive to stay alive and healthy—so we can eat!

Tassos C. Kyriakides, PhD, is an epidemiologist and biostatistician at Yale University's School of Public Health and School of Medicine, and a senior biostatistician at the Department of Veterans' Affairs Cooperative Studies Program. He has worked on multiple clinical research projects and has delivered numerous seminars and lectures in academic, scientific, research, and clinical settings. In addition, he explores the history, culture, and evidence-based science behind the beneficial impact of Greek and Mediterranean nutrition on human health.

INTRODUCTION

FOOD DEFINES ME AS A PERSON. IT ALWAYS HAS. AS THE SON OF GREEK immigrants, I grew up in a home where preparing and enjoying meals was among the most important times of the day. I went out to become a chef and run several restaurants, and so I've quite literally relied on food for my livelihood and thus my life. But over the years, I began to use food as a method to cope and surrender, mourn and rejoice, avoid and confront. I unknowingly started to hide behind it, and use it in ways that went beyond nourishing my body and soul. My weight fluctuated like crazy: At any given time, you could tell how stressed or overworked I was just by how heavy I was. But then I would lose those extra pounds when things leveled off. How could something that had brought me so much joy, fame, and success become the very thing I would struggle with for almost two decades?

I wrote this book because I needed a plan. I didn't want to be on a diet, because the word *diet* connotes one thing: deprivation. I don't know anyone who enjoys longing, especially for food. It's no surprise that diets fail. The Mediterranean diet, however, refers to a healthier approach to eating, one in which food is prepared using intensely flavorful, inherently healthful ingredients that satisfy. It is almost as simple as that. The thing that separates the Mediterranean diet from all others—and will keep you eating well and improving your health—is that it just tastes good.

For me, it only seemed natural to revisit the eating habits of my forebears, whose meals were based heavily on vegetables and fruits, whole grains, legumes and nuts, and healthy fats like olive oil. The Mediterranean diet emphasizes herbs and spices to flavor food, and features more fish and poultry than red meat. Pasta, that great American dinner fallback, is always a side dish—the portion size is meant as an accompaniment, not as the centerpiece of the meal. Drinking red wine in moderation is also part of the plan—as is enjoying the preparation and sharing of meals with family and friends. This last part, to my mind, is key.

As parents to two young boys, my wife, Anna, and I are painfully aware of how easy it is to let weeknight dinners become frantic, last-minute, and ultimately unsatisfying affairs. If part of a healthful eating plan is in the enjoyment of preparing the meals you eat, then this kind of frenzy guarantees the opposite. How could we make cooking healthful food at home a joyful experience for all of us, without resorting to gimmicks and false promises? In my restaurants, I enjoy the luxury of working with prep cooks who chop, peel, grate, pit, and otherwise make cooking for our guests a sheer pleasure because I have every prepped ingredient I need at my fingertips. What if Anna had only to reach into the refrigerator to get items that would transform not only *how* she cooked (more efficiently), but *what* she cooked (inherently healthy meals)? That would change the way she cooked and it would make sure that busy weeknights didn't get in the way of providing healthy meals for our family.

That's just what this book allows you to do. I have identified essential ingredients and techniques that make cooking modern Mediterranean food—and other ethnic foods translated through the Mediterranean diet—easy. If you spend a little time at the beginning of the week—we do it on Sundays—the prep you do then will pay huge dividends, providing stunning, easy meals for a week or two.

I went back to my roots to uncover those transformative ingredients and pantry items. I kept returning to the same seven things: Greek yogurt, shocked and blanched vegetables, sweet and sour peppers and onions, roasted cherry tomatoes, garlic confit, tomato sauce, and red wine vinaigrette. I developed a weekend ritual at home, preparing the staples according to the meals Anna had planned (and in some cases hadn't planned) for the week. I thought like a chef, but in my home kitchen. I created accessible, easily recognizable recipes that use these intensely flavorful Mediterranean staples in new and unusual ways.

Anna, a novice cook, was finding pleasure and satisfaction in the scrum that is making a weeknight dinner. We were all eating much more healthfully, and we were able to keep doing this for months without ever looking back. The plan works beautifully. After all, it is a way of eating that never once conjures the thought of deprivation, nor does it require special skills, equipment, or ingredients. And it puts an end to a catch-as-catch-can approach to cooking. No more 3:00 p.m. web searches for a dinner recipe that requires a trip to the store for an ingredient you may only use a fraction of. What this book does ask of you is a little preparation—maybe every few weeks—of the essentials. (See page 9 for a guide to get you started.)

Once you start prepping and cooking from the following pages, you will start cooking spontaneously, and reaching for the garlic puree instead of butter will become rote, Greek yogurt will become your go-to dairy product, and you'll realize just how much better—and more delicious—life is when there are partially cooked vegetables, roasted tomatoes, tomato sauce, and red wine vinaigrette in the refrigerator. That's what the plan delivers. I also hope that you come to a truth about cooking that only occurred to me on the death of my father, eight years ago: Food is not art. It is a means to share the joy of human company, conversation, and life. In our chaotic world, we need to find the time to create the everlasting memories of a simple shared meal. It provides the foundation of these wonderful moments in the healthiest possible way. That's why I called this book *Live to Eat*.

4

THE MAGNIFICENT SEVEN

LIVE TO EAT BUILDS ON SEVEN KEY PANTRY ITEMS THAT WILL CHANGE not only *what you eat,* but *the way you cook.* When I have blanched broccoli or roasted cherry tomatoes in my refrigerator, it feels like money in the culinary bank. With ingredients like this on hand, the dinner plan is practically set.

Why these particular seven? My goal was to deliver the greatest depth of flavor in the simplest possible way and to make it easy to incorporate healthy ingredients into your everyday cooking. Some of these essentials are a cinch to make, others require a little bit more effort, while still others take time, but very little of it is active. While I don't expect you to have all seven on hand at the same time, my bet is that you will come to find that there are some you can't live without. Note that the recipes make seemingly large quantities; the point is not for you to eat, say, onions and peppers for a week straight, but rather for you to enjoy them in one or two dishes and then freeze the rest—because I guarantee you will want those onions and peppers again.

Greek Yogurt—I do not offer a recipe for Greek yogurt itself, simply because there are very good commercial brands readily available in the supermarket. I *do* offer three additional recipes that utilize Greek yogurt in flavor-packed ways. To make Garlic Yogurt Sauce (page 31), add garlic and vinegar to plain yogurt. Add chiles in adobo to make Chipotle Yogurt Sauce (page 51), and cucumbers and dill to make Cucumber Yogurt Dip (tzatziki; page 36), which I use liberally throughout the book. (If you are lucky enough to live near a

Middle Eastern grocery or specialty food market, you will likely be able to find a quality prepared version of tzatziki. By all means, buy it!)

Make both Garlic Yogurt Sauce and Cucumber Yogurt Dip once a month. Prepare the Chipotle Yogurt Sauce as needed, since it requires only the addition of chiles in adobo to the Garlic Yogurt Sauce. None of the yogurt-based mixtures freeze well; but they will keep, in rigid containers with tight-fitting lids, in the refrigerator for up to 1 month.

Garden Vegetables and Fruits—If you have vegetables and fruit prepared and ready to go—into frittatas, pastas, and salads, and as side dishes—you're guaranteed to put something healthy on your plate. Blanching and shocking vegetables is a great technique to speed up dinner prep; they need only be warmed before serving. Ignore any temptation to use commercial frozen versions of these vegetables; there is no comparison—in texture, taste, and nutrients—to fresh vegetables. That said, I usually blanch and shock extra of everything and freeze it, which is quite different from the stuff you get in the freezer aisle.

I always prepare at least two vegetables every week and generally reserve a little time on Sunday to do it. To store: Drain thoroughly by laying the vegetables out on paper towels to absorb residual moisture (the enemy of any stored vegetable or fruit) and store in rigid containers. They'll keep for up to a week in the refrigerator. To freeze, transfer to resealable plastic freezer bags and seal, pressing on the bag to release any trapped air. The vegetables will keep in the freezer for up to 3 weeks. Prepared seasonal fruit—citrus that has been peeled, the pith removed, and the fruit sectioned; washed berries—guarantees that you'll reach for them when topping granola or yogurt, or when looking for an easy, healthful dessert.

Sweet and Sour Peppers and Onions—My favorite dip is made with sautéed peppers and onions, which is an excellent example of how the most basic, readily available ingredients—onions, peppers, garlic, white wine vinegar, and honey—can become something else altogether when gently sautéed and seasoned well. I make this in large quantities (because I *love* the vegetable dip for which it is the foundation) once a month. I'm not suggesting that you make two weeks of dinner using onions and peppers (but maybe you'll want to!), but because there is a bit of chopping, I'd rather go big, then freeze some to have on hand. Think through which dishes you will want to make with it over the course of two weeks and portion that amount into a rigid plastic container with a tight-fitting lid and refrigerate. Spoon the remaining into resealable plastic freezer bags in ½- to 1-cup portions. Press on the bag while sealing to release air pockets. Mark with the date and freeze for up to 1 month.

Roasted Cherry Tomatoes—Could. Not. Be. Easier. Toss in olive oil, season (with oregano, garlic, salt, and pepper), and pop into the oven for about 10 minutes. Toss the flavor-packed tomatoes with olives and potatoes for an instant side dish, whir in the blender with almonds to make a deeply flavorful pesto, and use them to make a rustic sauce for pasta. Eat them as a snack!

I roast cherry tomatoes once a week, right after I take the garlic confit out of the oven. Turn the heat up to 350°F and by the time the confit is cool enough to transfer to a container, the tomatoes will be done. To store, transfer the tomatoes and all of the pan juices (scrape up every last bit) into a rigid container with a tight-fitting lid and refrigerate for up to 1 week.

Garlic Confit—If you're going to make only one of the Magnificent Seven, make it this. There isn't a day that I don't dip into a container of garlic confit. Yes, to properly confit raw garlic—braising it in good olive oil—takes time, but most of the cooking time is passive. A quick hint: Purchase peeled garlic and save yourself the chore of peeling and an incredible amount of time.

I make confit once a week—on the same day that I blanch and shock my vegetables. First thing, get the garlic cloves into the oven, then start blanching and shocking your vegetables. The confit keeps, refrigerated, for up to 1 month.

Tomato Sauce—My recipe yields 3 quarts of sauce, which may seem like way too much, but the amount is intentional because tomato sauce freezes beautifully. Make this once a month, on a day when you have other projects that keep you in the house, as it requires very little preparation but a low, slow simmer (about 1½ hours). You can do this in the evening when you sit down to watch TV, walk on the treadmill, or read a book. No reason to stand over it watching the slow boil. To store, transfer what you plan to use over the course of a week or so into a rigid container with a tight-fitting lid and refrigerate for up to 1 week. Pour the remaining (cooled) sauce into resealable plastic freezer bags in 1- or 2-cup portions. Date and freeze for up to 6 months.

If you find yourself without this tomato sauce on hand, it's okay to use a top-quality jarred sauce, preferably one that you know and love. You can flavor it with a little red wine vinegar and additional spices if necessary. Use the recipe on page 174 as a guide.

Red Wine Vinaigrette—I can't live without this and neither should you. Pureed garlic confit, raw garlic, oregano, and mustard flavor my vinaigrette, which is extra-acidic so that its sprightliness is never blunted by other assertive ingredients in a dish. My recipe yields 3 cups (whirred together in seconds in a blender), which may seem excessive, except for the fact that it keeps forever. Make it once a month. My hope is that you use it above and beyond the recipes in the chapter—drizzled on mixed greens, tossed with steamed vegetables, brushed onto sandwich bread—and that it becomes a go-to flavor layer in all of your cooking. Store the vinaigrette in a rigid container with a tight-fitting lid.

While I am partial to my homemade vinaigrette, it is another example of an essential that can be purchased ready-made in a pinch. Choose a top-quality version, always seeking out organic, natural ingredients that you recognize when reading the label.

HOW TO USE THIS BOOK

WHENEVER I'M PLANNING A NEW RESTAURANT, I WRITE THREE WORDS AT the top of a page: *Crawl. Walk. Run.* All I've ever wanted to do is *run*, but I learned the hard way that shooting out of the gate brings burnout with it. I urge you to repeat those same three words as you adopt the Live to Eat method of cooking. If you follow the recipes in the order they appear in each chapter, you will see that they build on each other.

This book is not organized in a traditional way, with all of the appetizers in one section, main dishes in another, salads in another. I purposely arranged the recipes according to the essential ingredient they showcase. This way, you will learn how to use one ingredient (which can be prepared ahead) in a stunning variety of dishes.

Let's take Greek yogurt, which provides a beautiful example of how one ingredient can become the building block for dozens of meals—the Live to Eat method. In the first few recipes, I use it in parfaits and as a spread on smoked salmon sandwiches. When you add a little vinegar, it becomes a zingy dressing for drizzling over beets or tossing into salads. Add garlic confit, cucumbers, and dill, and Greek yogurt becomes a dip for vegetables, a spread for turkey burgers, a mayo replacement in chicken salad, and a flavor boost for sushi. Add a little chiles and adobo sauce to the dip and you have a spicy sauce for tacos, a spread for a spicy chicken sandwich, and a sauce for roasted salmon.

And those are just the dishes I suggest—you may be inspired to create your own. I have also included a second listing of all the recipes, organized by meal and type of dish, on pages viii–xiii, if you prefer the more traditional cookbook approach.

Flip through the cookbook, before you get started, to see what interests you. Then pick a recipe and determine which essentials you need to make it. You will find that some recipes require only one or two staples, while others may include four. My assumption is that you will always have Garlic Confit and Red Wine Vinaigrette on hand—because both last so long in the refrigerator!

I will know I have succeeded in converting you to my plan if you start to depart from my recipes, to deviate from them as befits your mood, your budget, and what's in the refrigerator. I want to release you from the tyranny of the recipe, which is why I've written these instructions in a very casual, conversational way. In general, I am reluctant to quote exact cooking times but would rather give you visual cues for the simple reason that no two stoves are the same, the quality of cooking equipment varies, and gas, electric, and convection ovens cook differently. Learning to cook by look and feel is always far more accurate than any timer or temperature gauge.

There are a few tools I consider essential to my life as a professional cook. You'll depend on them at home, too: a sharp knife, a mandoline slicer, a Microplane grater, a large rubber cutting board, a Vitamix or other high-powered blender, and heavy-bottomed pots and pans.

One last note: Read through the recipes completely before you begin; the last thing you want to encounter is the need for Tomato Sauce at 6 p.m. on a Tuesday night! That said, you don't have to make everything from scratch. I'm all for you using top-quality purchased versions of tomato sauce and red wine vinaigrette; just season them to taste as you would if you were making them from scratch. If you are lucky enough to live near a good Middle Eastern market, there's a good chance you will find excellent cucumber yogurt dip (tzatziki), which is made with Greek yogurt.

A FEW GOOD TECHNIQUES AND TIPS

I HAVE BEEN COOKING FOR SO LONG THAT IT IS EASY TO TAKE FOR GRANTED the skills and techniques I use in the kitchen every single day—both at work and at home. This came into especially sharp relief when I began preparing family meals with Anna, who did not grow up cooking. She would ask me to slow down or stop altogether while preparing dinner so that she could really master segmenting fruit, or understand how I make randomly chopped beets look good.

What follows are the techniques I returned to over and over while creating the recipes for this book. Take the time to learn them and soon enough they will become second nature to you, too.

Chopping—Knowing how to chop properly can considerably cut down on preparation time. A sharp kitchen knife is key, of course. But there's more to it than that. Every chef knows that presentation is wildly important—it's the first impression a diner gets and it matters. Which is why I have always chopped vegetables in a rather organic way, turning them a bit with each chop to create irregular shapes (but not irregular sizes). I have never been a fan of tomatoes cut into wedges or beets sliced into thick rounds—neither are the most appetizing ways to present these wonderful vegetables.

A tip: If you're a righty, begin chopping to the far right of the chopping board and work to the left so that you avoid the temptation to scrape the chopped vegetables away with your knife, which dulls it. If you're a lefty, do the opposite.

Beets: To chop a beet into bite-sized chunks, first trim and discard the ends. Cut the beet in half lengthwise and chop into ½-inch pieces, turning the beet slightly after each cut so that the pieces are not uniform in shape.

Tomatoes: Halve the tomato lengthwise and core, leaving the seeds in. Place the tomato, skin side down, on the cutting board and chop into ½-inch pieces, turning the tomato slightly after each cut so that the pieces are not uniform in shape.

Onions: My unorthodox technique for chopping onions wouldn't fly at Le Cordon Bleu, but it goes much faster once you get it down!

To cut onions into slivers, trim the ends and halve lengthwise. Peel away the papery skin. Lay an onion half, cut side down, on the cutting board with a trimmed end facing you. Working from one side to the other, slice the onion into ⅛-inch-thick slices.

To dice an onion, trim the ends and halve lengthwise. Peel away the papery skin. Place an onion half, cut side down, on a cutting board, with the trimmed ends on the left and right. Working from one end to the other, cut the onion into ¼-inch-thick slices. Turn the onion so that a trimmed end is facing you and working from one side to the other, slice again ¼ inch thick, creating ¼-inch dice. As you reach the halfway mark, turn the onion on its side and work from right to left again.

Peppers: All bell peppers—red, green, orange, yellow—are fairly uniform in shape. They are cut depending on how they are used in a recipe. For example, I cut them into strips to make Sweet and Sour Peppers and Onions (page 94) and matchsticks when serving raw with dip as in Cucumber Yogurt Dip with Crudités and Warm Pita (page 39).

To cut into strips, trim closely to the root and stem ends and discard. Remove the pith and seeds entirely (if you hit a seed while chopping it can cause the knife to slip) and place on the cutting board, skin side down. Cut lengthwise into the flesh side into ½-inch-thick strips. To cut into matchsticks, trim the root and stem end more generously so that the pepper resembles a cylinder and proceed as above.

Sectioning Citrus—To section oranges, grapefruits, and lemons, first trim the ends and set a cut side on a cutting board. Using a sharp knife, trim away the peel and pith, making curved vertical cuts into the fruit and working around it until the sections are exposed. Then, working over a bowl to catch the juices,

hold the fruit in the palm of your hand and cut into each section with a sharp knife to release it from the membrane and into the bowl. Squeeze the membrane of all its juices and discard.

Juicing Lemons—Trim the ends of the lemon and stand it up on one end on a cutting board. Using a sharp knife, remove the pithy core in the middle by cutting a triangle around it. Use the tip of the knife to remove the seeds. Squeeze.

Preparing Watermelon—To prepare a whole watermelon, I like to cut it into quarters lengthwise to make cutting uniform triangles easier.

First, trim the ends with a sharp knife. Stand the watermelon on one end on a cutting board. Making curved vertical cuts, trim away the rind, including the white part. Halve the watermelon lengthwise, then cut each half in two lengthwise. Cut the fruit crosswise into ¾-inch-thick triangles.

If you only need part of the watermelon, cut what you need without removing the rind and wrap the exposed area of the remaining watermelon in plastic. Trim away the cut sides of the watermelon if they seem to be going south, which can happen even if it is tightly covered in plastic wrap.

Preparing Herbs—Throughout, I call for chopped mixed herbs, which means dill, mint, and parsley. It is invaluable to have a stash of these ready and waiting in the refrigerator so that all that's required are a quick chop and a sprinkling. You can throw them into a pasta in the dead of winter and it's as if you threw open the windows for spring.

To prepare herb bunches, pull them apart, wash, and lay out on paper towels as above. Once completely dry (water is an enemy to fresh herbs), roll the individual bunches in paper towels and label directly on the towel. Slide the rolls into a resealable plastic bag and refrigerate. This big bag of herbs, referred to as *the pillow* in my house, is one key to bright flavor. Each time you use the herbs, replace the paper towel.

Prepping a Grill—No matter what you are doing when it comes to grilling, you must preheat. This way you are searing whatever you are putting on it, which seals in the flavor. This goes for vegetables as well as meat. If you preheat the grill properly, your food won't stick.

If you have a cast-iron grate on your grill, heating it will burn off all the bits left behind from last time. If you want to season the grate, brush up and down with a blend of canola and olive oil. It's just like seasoning a cast-iron pan. If the grates are stainless steel, brush them down as you would a stainless-steel pan, using soapy water and a Brillo Pad. If using a grill pan, be sure that it is clean and well-seasoned. Most important: make sure your exhaust fan is turned on! I love the smoky smell but my wife doesn't.

Storing and Freezing—As you have gathered by now, preparation is key to the Live to Eat approach. Having what you need at your fingertips makes cooking so much more pleasurable, and that goes not only for ingredients and tools, but the containers and lids and freezer bags that keep you organized and your food as fresh as possible. Fill a kitchen drawer with the following:

Rigid storage containers: There are so many options out there it can be overwhelming. Clear is key. Glass or plastic, whichever you prefer, but be sure the lids fit securely; air and water are the enemy. I am partial to quart-size plastic containers. We use them to store dozens of items in the restaurant; buy a sleeve of them, along with painter's tape (it is removable and leaves no residue) for marking the contents and you will be very happy. I also love OXO "POP" storage containers: When you press the button on the lid, it pushes out any air inside the container, which helps to keep the contents fresher, longer. They have wide mouths, which gives you easy, full access to the contents and are stackable.

Resealable plastic freezer bags: You can't have enough of these. Not only are they easy to work with, but they are the most efficient, space-wise, for storage. Always date the items you freeze; a two-year-old frozen tomato sauce will not deliver on the Live to Eat promise.

GREEK YOGURT

GREEK YOGURT

GREEK YOGURT IS AS ESSENTIAL TO THE MEDITERRANEAN KITCHEN AS OLIVES and feta cheese. It is always on hand, in the way that every refrigerator in America is never without mayonnaise and butter. The thick Greek yogurt I snacked on as a kid, it turns out, opened culinary doors for me when I began to incorporate it into the dishes I made in fine restaurants. Its intensely piquant flavor—it can be funky (cow's milk) or grassy (sheep or goat's milk)—makes a wonderful, bright substitution for ingredients from a chef's standard dairy larder: cream cheese, heavy cream, mayonnaise, butter, sour cream, and crème fraîche. Other chefs took note and began using this "new" ingredient to lighten and brighten their dishes.

Back then, I was more taken with the flavor and texture of Greek yogurt than with its health benefits. I was cooking the way I'd eaten my whole life. But with Mediterranean cooking, flavor and healthy eating are entwined.

In this chapter, you'll come to understand the beauty, versatility, and inherently healthful benefits of Greek yogurt; my hope is that you will keep it in your refrigerator at all times—right next to the butter, ketchup, and mayo so that

replacing those fatty, sugary staples becomes reflexive. The recipes that follow are recognizable, approachable, and inherently good for you because I've used a Mediterranean approach. Skip the mayonnaise to bind your egg salad and use Greek yogurt instead. Do the same on a tuna melt. Spread it onto a turkey burger and skip the ketchup altogether.

More than in any other chapter in this book, this one beautifully demonstrates the Live to Eat method of building on one ingredient to make several others. Greek yogurt is the base upon which several dips, sauces, and spreads are created simply by adding a little garlic and a spice, or flavorful liquid, or chopped vegetables.

For example, the chapter begins with recipes calling for straight Greek yogurt simply combined with smoked salmon, or berries and granola, or berries and seeds. Or you can add a little garlic and vinegar to yogurt to make the briny Garlic Yogurt Sauce (page 31) for drizzling over beets or binding egg salad. When you add cucumbers, garlic, vinegar, and dill to the same Greek yogurt, you make the multi-tasking Cucumber Yogurt Dip (page 36), also known as *tzatziki*, that is great for spreading on sandwiches, dipping vegetables into, or spooning onto meats and poultry. And finally, add a little heat with chipotle peppers to create a Chipotle Yogurt Sauce (page 51) that stands up to grilled fish and meat.

The homemade yogurt I grew up with tasted like no other, but these days, there's no need to make your own. My preferred brands are full-fat Fage and Skotidakis, which both come close to the creamy texture and rich flavor of homemade. I highly recommend seeking out either of these in their full-fat form (reduced fat versions won't satisfy the same way), but whatever brand you choose (and there are dozens now), be sure it has the consistency of cream cheese. If a spoon won't stand straight up by itself then it's not *real* Greek yogurt. The next best thing to good Greek yogurt is to strain regular, plain full-fat yogurt: Line a colander with cheesecloth and set it over a bowl. Spoon the yogurt into it, tie the cheesecloth tight, and refrigerate overnight. The next morning, the yogurt should be thick enough to stand a spoon up in.

It could not be more straightforward: Whenever you find yourself reaching for the cream cheese, packaged fruited *yogurt*, or frozen yogurt, catch yourself and grab the *full-fat, plain Greek yogurt* instead. When spread on a whole grain English muffin and draped with lox, it is a perfect Live to Eat makeover of that Sunday brunch staple, bagels and lox. Good-quality Greek yogurt is delicious straight off the spoon, which makes it ideal for topping with granola, berries, nuts, and seeds. But if you mix it with sugar-loaded pre-packaged granolas, it defeats the point. (Most granola—despite the healthy reputation—is loaded with sugar because it helps hold the stuff together and makes it crunchy, which is, of course, the best part. Read labels scrupulously; if there is high-fructose corn syrup and/or the second ingredient is sugar, move on. I go for flax seed granola and drizzle my own honey over it. But a handful of seeds and a drizzle of honey get you the same effect—and *you* control the amount of sugar.)

Think of Greek yogurt as you might frozen yogurt; top it with fresh berries and you have a far healthier treat (or breakfast or dessert) than any Pinkberry concoction. And that's the point. Greek yogurt, all on its own, is a culinary chameleon—and my hope is that it becomes as natural a choice for you as it is for me.

WITH GREEK YOGURT IN YOUR REFRIGERATOR, YOU CAN MAKE:

OPEN-FACED SMOKED SALMON SANDWICHES

Makes 4

The recipe can easily be scaled up—doubled, tripled—to feed a crowd. It's not essential to use a mandoline to slice the onions, but it will get you the thinnest rings possible. Their texture will be softer and they will enhance—rather than over-power—the other ingredients.

2 whole grain English muffins, split and toasted

½ cup Greek yogurt

4 ounces smoked salmon, cut into paper-thin slices

2 large beefsteak tomatoes (preferably yellow), cut into ¼-inch-thick slices

½ small red onion, cut into paper-thin slices

1 cup packed arugula

4 teaspoons chopped fresh dill

1 teaspoon extra virgin olive oil

Kosher salt

Fresh ground black pepper

Spread each English muffin half with some of the yogurt. Arrange the smoked salmon on the muffin and top with the tomatoes, red onion, arugula, and dill. Drizzle with olive oil and season with salt and pepper to taste.

YOGURT WITH BERRIES AND SEEDS

Serves 4

I use equal amounts of each seed, but feel free to combine them in any proportion that suits you. Whenever you crave crunch, pull out this healthy combination. Make a double batch of it and store it in an airtight container; it will keep at least 3 months.

2 teaspoons shelled sunflower seeds
2 teaspoons pumpkin seeds
2 teaspoons chia seeds
2 teaspoons flax seeds
1½ cups Greek yogurt
¼ cup clover honey
2 cups mixed berries (blackberries, blueberries, raspberries)

Combine the seeds in a small bowl and mix thoroughly.

Divide the yogurt among four glasses. Drizzle the honey among them, followed by half of the seeds. Divide the fruit among the glasses, then top with the remaining seed mix.

MIX IT UP

The next two recipes use Pistachio Butter to add heft to these parfaits, but you can mix Greek yogurt with anything. Try it with citrus supremes and mint (as on page 89), or with any mix of fruits, seeds, and nut butters you have at home.

YOGURT PARFAITS WITH GRANOLA AND PISTACHIO BUTTER

Serves 4

Salty, smooth Pistachio Butter, made from mixing the nuts with fruity olive oil in a blender (yes, it's that easy) is insanely delicious—not only on yogurt, but as a sauce with gamy meats such as lamb and venison.

2 cups Greek yogurt
½ cup Pistachio Butter (below)
½ cup clover honey
2 cups organic flax seed granola

Divide 1 cup of the yogurt among four 8-ounce glasses. Drizzle half of the Pistachio Butter among each, followed by half of the honey and half of the granola. Repeat, ending with the granola.

PISTACHIO BUTTER

Makes ½ cup

You must have a powerful blender, otherwise pureeing the pistachio nuts will be a challenge. They must become a smooth butter or it will be an oily mess that I do not recommend for yogurt.

1 cup whole unsalted pistachios, shelled
5 tablespoons extra virgin olive oil
½ teaspoon kosher salt
Pinch fresh ground black pepper

Pulse the pistachios in a blender until finely ground. Add the oil and blend until smooth. Season with salt and pepper. The Pistachio Butter will keep, tightly covered, for up to 3 months. (Do not store in the refrigerator.)

NOTE: Vitamix makes the standard industrial blender used in professional kitchens. They are not cheap but are well worth the investment for a serious home cook. They make a great gift!

YOGURT PARFAITS WITH STEWED STRAWBERRIES AND PISTACHIO BUTTER

Serves 4

Once berries are stewed, it's just as easy to make a parfait as it is to grab a preservative-loaded treat from the freezer. As you stew the berries, watch the honey-cinnamon syrup carefully as it reduces in the saucepan—it thickens quickly. Store in the refrigerator in an airtight container for 2 weeks.

⅓ cup clover honey

1 cinnamon stick

12 strawberries, hulled and cut lengthwise into ¼-inch-thick slices

¼ cup Pistachio Butter (optional; page 27)

1½ cups Greek yogurt

Prepare an ice bath. Combine the honey, cinnamon stick, and 2 cups water in a saucepan and bring to a boil. Reduce the heat and simmer until the liquid reduces enough that it just coats the bottom of the pan. Add the strawberries and cook until a fork easily pierces them, 5 to 8 minutes. Set the pan in the ice bath and let cool completely.

Layer the ingredients in four tall clear glasses. If not using butter, add nuts, granola, or seeds for some crunch.

NOTE: This dish, as with all the other parfaits, is a great dessert to end a killer meal—just enough sweet but not cloying—but it is also a great way to start the day. Kids will love it!

GARLIC YOGURT SAUCE

Makes 2½ cups

This sauce, as simple as adding vinegar and a bit of fresh garlic to Greek yogurt, adds zing to almost any vegetable, sandwich, or grilled meat or poultry. Skip the mayo, reach for this sauce, and use it to give a healthy makeover to that classic American combination of hard-boiled eggs, mayonnaise, and a dollop of mustard. Or drizzle it over good-quality pickled beets and an instant side dish (with a delectable dressing that develops when the sauce mixes with the brine) is born. If you have blanched and shocked vegetables (see page 62) on hand, yet another side dish can be ready in minutes. The sauce, which has the consistency of pudding, will firm up in the refrigerator. To loosen it up, gradually stir in up to ¼ cup milk.

2 cloves garlic, peeled
¼ cup white vinegar or white wine
　vinegar
2 cups Greek yogurt
Kosher salt
Fresh ground black pepper

In a blender, blend the garlic and vinegar on medium speed until smooth; no chunks of garlic should be visible. Transfer to a bowl, add the yogurt, and whisk until smooth. Season with salt and pepper and whisk again. Use immediately or transfer to a container with a tight-fitting lid and refrigerate for up to 2 weeks.

NOTE: This is shockingly good on grilled vegetables and meats. It takes the simple and creates something special that you may call your own. Your friends will be awed!

PICKLED BEETS WITH GARLIC YOGURT SAUCE

Serves 4

Toss briny beets in olive oil and you are essentially making a vinaigrette. The sauce rounds it out with a little richness.

2 large jarred pickled beets, cut into
   1-inch pieces, excess liquid removed
¼ cup extra virgin olive oil
Kosher salt
Fresh ground black pepper
**½ to ¾ cup Garlic Yogurt Sauce
  (page 31)**
2 tablespoons chopped mixed fresh
  herbs (dill, parsley, mint)
2 tablespoons crushed smoked
  almonds

Combine the beets and olive oil in a medium bowl and toss to thoroughly coat. Season with salt and pepper. Transfer the dressed beets to a serving bowl and spoon the yogurt sauce over them. Sprinkle the herbs and almonds on top and serve.

NOTE: I like to cut beets and other vegetables, like tomatoes for a salad, into random shapes rather than perfect wedges or cubes. The irregular shapes make for a more appealing visual result. To prevent staining your cutting board, put down a piece of parchment paper before slicing the beets.

GREEK YOGURT

Serves 4

This is one of our most popular dishes at MP Taverna and quite easy to make at home—especially if you've followed my method of prepping vegetables for a week at a time.

2 large jarred pickled beets, cut into ½-inch pieces (see page 11)

2 tablespoons extra virgin olive oil

Kosher salt

Fresh ground black pepper

½ pound haricots verts, blanched and shocked (see page 62)

½ medium fennel bulb, sliced paper thin on a mandoline or with very sharp knife

½ small red onion, cut crosswise into ⅛-inch-thick slices

6 tablespoons Red Wine Vinaigrette (page 192)

1 ruby red grapefruit, peeled, pith removed, and cut crosswise into ¼-inch-thick rounds

½ cup Garlic Yogurt Sauce (page 31)

2 tablespoons crushed smoked almonds, optional

Combine the beets and olive oil in a small bowl and toss to coat. Season with salt and pepper. Combine the haricots verts, fennel, and onion in a large bowl, add the vinaigrette, and toss.

Arrange the grapefruit slices on a serving platter and top with the beets. Spoon the yogurt sauce over them and top with the bean mixture. Scatter the almonds on top, if using, and serve.

CUCUMBER YOGURT DIP (TZATZIKI)

Makes 5½ cups

Greeks use this condiment, known as *tzatziki*, on just about everything. If you are lucky enough to find the authentic prepared stuff, go ahead and buy it. Either way, you will have a seriously flavorful and healthy sauce.

This recipe yields far more than you'll need to make any one dish, which is the point. If you have it on hand, it will take you less than 30 minutes to make most of the other dishes in this chapter. It's a dip for vegetables and pita, a flavor-packed sauce for sushi (yes, it's easier to make than you think—and it doesn't have to be perfectly executed to taste amazing), yet another replacement (along with Garlic Yogurt Sauce, page 31) for mayonnaise in chicken, tuna, crab, or egg salad sandwiches (or any sandwich that calls for mayonnaise), and a condiment for grilled meat, poultry, and fish.

3 cloves garlic, peeled or
Garlic Confit (page 138)
½ cup white vinegar or white wine
vinegar
4 cups Greek yogurt
1 large English cucumber, ends
trimmed, peeled, and halved
lengthwise, seeds discarded and
flesh cut into ¼-inch dice
3 tablespoons loosely packed
chopped fresh dill
2 teaspoons kosher salt
¼ teaspoon fresh ground black pepper

Combine garlic and vinegar in a blender and puree until smooth. Combine the yogurt and garlicky vinegar in a bowl. Using a whisk, gently work the liquid into the yogurt until it is fully incorporated.

Fold in the cucumbers, dill, salt, and pepper. Transfer to a container with a tight-fitting lid. The dip will keep for up to 1 week in the refrigerator.

NOTE: Be sure to remove all of the seeds from the cucumber; they release water, which will make the dip too loose.

If raw garlic is too assertive for you, use the tamer, sweeter Garlic Confit (page 138).

I love the almost obnoxiously acidic flavor of white vinegar here, but you can tone it down by using white wine vinegar instead.

WITH CUCUMBER YOGURT DIP IN YOUR REFRIGERATOR, YOU CAN MAKE:

Serves 4 to 6

The more interesting the vegetables, the more interesting the dish—but baby peeled carrots will also do the trick.

2 rounds whole wheat pita
1½ cups Cucumber Yogurt Dip (page 37) or store-bought tzatziki
1 tablespoon extra virgin olive oil
Pinch fresh ground black pepper
2 pounds mixed fresh vegetables such as carrots, celery, broccoli, grape tomatoes, and peppers, cut into matchsticks or bite-sized pieces

Warm the pitas in a microwave or toaster for a crunchier texture. Alternatively, to add a smoky flavor, place directly over a gas flame until very lightly charred in places. Flip over and repeat on the other side. Stack the pitas on top of each other and cut into eighths.

Put the dip into a serving bowl, drizzle the olive oil on top, and season with the pepper. Serve with the vegetables and pita.

NOTE: Give this to your kids to dip their tortilla chips and pretzels in. It gets them one step closer to liking yogurt.

SALMON SUSHI WITH CUCUMBER YOGURT DIP

Makes 20 pieces / Serves 4

Sushi-grade salmon is essential here—and you should buy it the day you plan to serve the sushi. It's okay if the slices are not all uniform; they don't have to look perfect to taste delicious.

1¼ cups Brown Sushi Rice (below)
4 ounces sushi-grade salmon, sliced against the grain on an angle into ¼-inch-thick slices
Extra virgin olive oil for rubbing
½ cup Cucumber Yogurt Dip (page 37) or store-bought tzatziki
Kosher salt
Fresh ground black pepper
Fresh dill fronds for garnish

Wet your hands and scoop 1 tablespoon of the rice into one palm. Make a fist around it to shape into a ½- x 1-inch rectangle. Push the ends in with your thumb and index finger to create clean edges. Put the rice block on a platter and repeat with remaining rice.

Drape a slice of salmon over each rectangle, then rub each slice with olive oil using your finger. Spoon a teaspoon of the yogurt dip onto each and season with salt and pepper. Garnish with the dill fronds and serve immediately.

NOTE: You must slice the fish against the grain (white fatty lines between flesh) for the correct texture.

BROWN SUSHI RICE

Makes 2 cups

1 cup short grain brown rice
1½ teaspoons canola oil
1 tablespoon red wine vinegar
½ teaspoon sugar
½ teaspoon kosher salt

Rinse the rice multiple times and drain thoroughly. Combine the rice with 2 cups cold water and the canola oil in a medium pot. Bring to a boil, then cover and reduce the heat to low. Cook until the liquid is absorbed, 40 to 45 minutes. Thoroughly stir in the vinegar, sugar, and salt and set aside to cool.

TUNA MELTS

Makes 4

I love this classic diner staple, but it is usually overloaded with mayonnaise and cheese and made with albacore or dark tuna fish, which is far less flavorful than unctuous yellowfin packed in oil. There should only be two ingredients listed on the jar or can of tuna: yellowfin tuna and olive oil.

10 ounces canned Italian tuna in oil, drained

½ cup Cucumber Yogurt Dip (page 37) or store-bought tzatziki

¼ medium red onion, diced

½ teaspoon fresh lemon juice

8 slices whole grain bread

4 slices Gruyère cheese or other melting cheese

4 leaves green leaf lettuce or Romaine, or ½ cup packed arugula or any leafy green

1 teaspoon extra virgin olive oil

2 tablespoons chopped mixed fresh herbs (dill, parsley, mint)

Kosher salt

Fresh ground black pepper

1 avocado, pitted and cut into ¼-inch-thick slices

Combine the tuna and dip in a bowl and fold together with a fork just until the tuna is nicely coated yet still chunky. Add the onion and ¼ teaspoon of the lemon juice and gently fold together.

Lightly toast the bread in a toaster oven or under the broiler. Place a slice of cheese on 4 of the slices and return to the oven to melt.

Meanwhile, toss the greens in the remaining ¼ teaspoon lemon juice and the olive oil. Toss in the herbs and season with salt and pepper. Divide the greens among the remaining 4 slices of bread. Scoop an equal amount of tuna over the greens, fan the avocado slices over, and top with the toasted cheese slices, cheese side down. Cut the sandwiches on the diagonal and serve.

NOTE: I like to toast the bread and melt the cheese first so the tuna and other ingredients remain at room temperature. They are textually brighter and so much fresher-looking.

GREEK TURKEY BURGERS

Makes 4

A generous tablespoon of garlic puree not only helps bind the ground turkey mixture, but is critical for adding moisture and a wonderful layer of flavor to the patties.

Extra virgin olive oil, for rubbing
¼ cup milk
2 slices whole wheat bread, crusts removed
1 pound ground turkey
1 heaping tablespoon Garlic Puree (page 141)
Kosher salt
Fresh ground black pepper
¼ cup Cucumber Yogurt Dip (page 37) or store-bought tzatziki
4 whole wheat English muffins, split and toasted
½ lemon
8 (¼-inch-thick) slices beefsteak tomato
8 thin-sliced red onion rings
½ cup packed arugula
3 tablespoons loosely packed chopped mixed herbs (dill, parsley, mint)

Line a small tray with parchment paper and rub it all over with olive oil.

Combine the milk with ¼ cup water in a large shallow bowl. Add the bread, using your hands to soak it. Squeeze out any excess liquid.

Combine the bread, turkey, and garlic puree in a medium bowl. Mix with your hands until just combined. Handle it as little as possible. Divide the mixture into 4 equal portions. Shape each portion into a ½-inch-thick patty, place on the tray, and rub olive oil over each.

Preheat a gas grill or grill pan over medium heat. Season both sides of each patty with salt and pepper, then grill until soft to the touch for burgers that are just cooked through.

Spread the dip on 4 of the English muffin halves. Top with a patty followed by a squeeze of lemon juice, 2 slices of tomato, red onion, arugula, herbs, a sprinkle of salt and pepper, and the muffin top.

VARIATION: BAKED TURKEY MEATBALLS

Preheat the oven to 375°F. Using a 1-ounce scoop, shape the turkey mixture into about 16 meatballs. Place on a baking sheet and brush with olive oil. Bake, turning once, until the turkey has lost all its pink color. To serve, toss in **Tomato Sauce (page 174),** serve simply with **Garlic Yogurt Sauce (page 31)** and a wedge of lemon, or stuff them into pita and dress with **Cucumber Yogurt Dip (page 37).**

GRILLED CHICKEN SALAD SANDWICHES

Makes 4

Here's another example (see Mediterranean Egg Salad Sandwiches, next page) of how a simple substitution of Cucumber Yogurt Dip for mayonnaise can transform a classic—and make it healthier.

2 (10-ounce) boneless, skinless chicken breasts
Kosher salt
Fresh ground black pepper
½ cup Cucumber Yogurt Dip (page 37) or store-bought tzatziki
4 whole grain bagels, halved, soft interiors scooped out and discarded
2 large beefsteak tomatoes, preferably yellow, sliced into ¼-inch-thick slices
½ small red onion, sliced into ¼-inch-thick slices
½ cup packed arugula
Juice of ½ lemon
4 roasted red pepper halves packed in oil, drained

Preheat a gas grill or grill pan over medium heat. Season each chicken breast with salt and pepper. Grill the breasts for 2 minutes on each side, or until they just lose their pink color, then transfer to a cutting board to rest for at least 2 minutes. Cut into ¼-inch pieces.

In a bowl, combine chicken and dip. Toss to thoroughly coat. Divide the mixture among 4 of the bagel halves. Arrange tomato slices over each and season with salt. Top each with red onion, followed by some arugula. Sprinkle with lemon juice, season with salt and pepper, and top each with a roasted red pepper. Top with the remaining bagel halves and serve.

NOTE: Grilled chicken breasts exemplify the beauty of the Live to Eat approach—grill extra and you will have a number of lunch and dinner options at your fingertips: Chop up and add to the Modern Greek Salad (page 195) or Traditional Greek Salad (page 196), or stuff into pita with some Cucumber Yogurt Dip (page 37). Or warm through and throw some Roasted Cherry Tomatoes (page 114) on top, or serve with blanched broccoli (see page 62) with a wedge of lemon and the Red Wine Vinaigrette (page 192). Grilling chicken on a charcoal or gas grill is ideal, but a grill pan is the next best thing.

MEDITERRANEAN EGG SALAD SANDWICHES

Makes 4

This is definitely one of my favorites. Greek yogurt replaces mayonnaise entirely, and only half of the egg yolks wind up in the mix here. Stuff into a pita with tomatoes and arugula and call it a healthy lunch.

8 hard-boiled eggs, whites and yolks
  separated, whites chopped into
  ½-inch pieces
½ cup Garlic Yogurt Sauce (page 31)
1 tablespoon Dijon mustard
Kosher salt
Fresh ground black pepper
¼ cup diced red onion
2 tablespoons capers, rinsed
  and drained
1 tablespoon chopped fresh dill
4 whole wheat pocket pitas, halved
3 medium beefsteak tomatoes
  (preferably yellow), cut into
  ¼-inch-thick slices
2 cups packed arugula

Combine egg yolks and yogurt sauce in a medium bowl and mash with a fork until smooth. Add the mustard and stir until incorporated. Season to taste with salt and pepper. Add the egg whites, onion, capers, and dill and fold gently to combine. Divide the egg salad among the pita halves and tuck some tomato slices and arugula into each.

NOTE: Add leftover potatoes to this for a killer potato-and-egg salad.

Serves 4

If you have Cucumber Yogurt Dip (page 37) or store-bought tzatziki on hand, you have this meal ready in the time it takes to grill the chicken. In Greece, souvlaki is usually served on skewers alongside French fries, but this is satisfying all on its own, so skip the potatoes and go with a salad instead.

The chunks of chicken should marinate in the ladolemono, a deeply flavorful garlic lemon oil, for at least 2 hours. Combine them in a resealable plastic bag in the morning so that by dinnertime the chicken is ready to grill.

1 pound boneless, skinless chicken breasts, cut into ½-inch cubes

½ cup Ladolemono (page 161)

4 (¼-inch-thick) sweet onion rings

2 teaspoons canola oil

½ cup Cucumber Yogurt Dip (page 37) or store-bought tzatziki

4 rounds whole wheat pita, warmed

2 beefsteak tomatoes, cut into 12 (¼-inch-thick) slices

1 good-quality roasted red pepper in oil, drained and cut into ¼-inch-thick strips

Kosher salt

Fresh ground black pepper

1 cup packed arugula

½ lemon

Combine the chicken with ¼ cup of the ladolemono in a resealable plastic bag, shake to coat, and refrigerate for at least 2 hours. Toss the onion rings in the canola oil.

Preheat a gas grill or grill pan over medium-high heat. Grill the chicken, taking care to keep the pieces from falling through the grate, turning once, until cooked through and the pieces are firm to the touch. At the same time, grill the onion rings until charred and softened. Transfer to a plate. Drizzle the remaining ladolemono over the chicken.

To assemble the souvlaki, spread 2 tablespoons of the dip down the middle of each pita. Arrange the chicken pieces over it, followed by onions, tomatoes, and peppers, dividing them equally. Season with salt and pepper. Top each with some arugula and squeeze lemon juice on top. Serve warm.

CHEF'S TRICK

When traditional souvlaki is on the menu at my restaurants—skewered with vegetables and served over rice—we never thread the chicken onto skewers before grilling. This eliminates the need to soak the wooden sticks. Instead, we slide the pieces onto the skewers after they are grilled, strictly for presentation. This isn't necessary, but it does make for a good-looking dish.

CHIPOTLE YOGURT SAUCE

Makes 1¼ cups

Smoky and spicy chipotle peppers plus Cucumber Yogurt Dip make for an entirely different condiment, one that you can use on almost anything that calls for mayonnaise or ketchup. If you take away anything from this chapter, note how a classic ethnic dish like tacos, which are traditionally loaded with sour cream and cheese, can be made healthier by swapping out the fattier ingredients for more healthful Mediterranean flavors. If you prefer a little heat you may substitute this sauce in any of the recipes in this chapter calling for Garlic Yogurt Sauce or Cucumber Yogurt Dip.

Chipotle peppers in adobo sauce are typically packed whole and come in a can. Once open, the peppers will keep, covered, in the refrigerator up to 1 month. If you can find them pureed, you're a hero. If not, blend them until they're nice and smooth before stirring into the yogurt.

1 cup Cucumber Yogurt Dip (page 37) or store-bought tzatziki
3 tablespoons pureed chipotle peppers in adobo sauce
Kosher salt
Fresh ground black pepper

Combine the yogurt and pureed peppers in a small bowl and stir until thoroughly combined. Season with salt and pepper. The sauce will keep, tightly covered, in the refrigerator for up to 2 weeks. Stir well before each use.

WITH CHIPOTLE YOGURT SAUCE IN YOUR REFRIGERATOR, YOU CAN MAKE:
Mediterranean Tacos (page 52)
Spicy Grilled Chicken Sandwiches with Chipotle Yogurt Sauce (page 54)
Spicy Roasted Salmon with Chipotle Yogurt Sauce (page 57)
Mediterranean Salsa (page 104)
Spicy Egg White Scramble (page 105)
Spicy Chicken Tacos (page 107)

MEDITERRANEAN TACOS

Makes 8 / Serves 4

Chipotle Yogurt Sauce replaces sour cream here, and ground chicken seasoned with my Gyro Spice Mix makes a lower fat alternative to beef.

2 tablespoons canola oil
½ medium yellow onion, cut into
  ¼-inch dice
1 pound ground chicken
Kosher salt
Fresh ground black pepper
2 tablespoons Gyro Spice Mix (recipe follows)
2 tablespoons tomato paste
2 roasted peppers in oil, drained and diced
2 tablespoons pureed chipotle peppers in adobo sauce, optional
½ medium red onion, cut into ¼-inch dice
1 small beefsteak tomato, preferably yellow, cut into ¼-inch dice
2 tablespoons Ladolemono (page 161); or substitute a squeeze of lemon or lime
2 tablespoons chopped fresh dill
½ cup Chipotle Yogurt Sauce (page 51)
8 (6-inch) corn or multigrain flour tortillas, wrapped in foil and warmed in a 200°F oven
Handful arugula

Heat the oil in a medium skillet over medium heat. Add the diced yellow onion and sauté until soft, fragrant, and glossy but not browned. Raise the heat to medium high, add the chicken, and season with salt and pepper. Brown the chicken, breaking it up with a spoon, until it is no longer pink. Stir in the spice mix until it is fragrant and evenly distributed. Stir in the tomato paste. Add 2 cups water to the mixture, bring to a boil, then reduce to a simmer. Cook until all of the liquid has evaporated, 10 to 15 minutes. Add the roasted peppers and, if desired, the pureed chipotle peppers.

Meanwhile, combine the red onion, tomato, and ladolemono in a small bowl and toss to coat. Season with salt and pepper and stir in the dill.

To compose each taco, spread 1 tablespoon of the chipotle sauce down the center of a tortilla. Spoon some chicken mixture over and top with some onion/tomato mixture. Top with arugula and serve warm.

VARIATION: Add some canned beans for a kickass chili and top with chipotle yogurt.

GYRO SPICE MIX

Makes about ¾ cup

This simple mix can be used to season any vegetable, protein, sauce, or vinaigrette. It's also a killer rub for roasted chicken or ribs or as a crust for quick-seared proteins like tuna.

¼ cup ground cumin
¼ cup ground cardamom
2 tablespoons cinnamon
1 tablespoon ground cloves
1 tablespoon fresh ground black pepper
2½ teaspoons kosher salt

Combine all of the ingredients in a jar with a tight-fitting lid. Stir with a spoon to thoroughly mix. The mixture will keep, tightly covered, for up to 3 months.

SPICY GRILLED CHICKEN SANDWICHES WITH CHIPOTLE YOGURT SAUCE

Makes 4

Pounding chicken breasts very thin before grilling not only cuts down on cooking time but guarantees even cooking. I like to cut the grilled chicken into very thin slices on a diagonal rather than leaving the pieces whole; it makes the sandwich more pleasant to eat and is reminiscent of a classic deli sandwich.

2 (10-ounce) boneless, skinless chicken breasts, or 2½ pounds pre-sliced chicken cutlets
Kosher salt
Fresh ground black pepper
2 tablespoons Spicy Red Rub (recipe follows)
4 whole grain ciabatta rolls, split horizontally
½ cup Chipotle Yogurt Sauce (page 51)
½ small red onion, cut into ¼-inch-thick slices
1 beefsteak tomato, preferably yellow, cut into ¼-inch-thick slices
1 avocado, halved, pitted, and cut into ¼-inch-thick slices

Preheat a gas grill or grill pan over medium heat. Working with one breast at a time, place it between two pieces of plastic wrap or parchment. Using the flat side of a meat tenderizer, pound the breast evenly to a ¼-inch thickness.

Season each chicken breast with some salt and pepper. Rub the spice mix onto the chicken, thoroughly coating both sides. Grill the breasts for 2 minutes on each side, until cooked through, then transfer to a cutting board to rest for at least 2 minutes. Cut the chicken crosswise into very thin slices, holding the knife on an angle.

To assemble the sandwiches, spread one half of each ciabatta with 2 tablespoons of the chipotle sauce. Arrange the sliced chicken on top, followed by the onion, tomato, and avocado, dividing them equally among the sandwich halves. Season with salt and pepper and top with the remaining ciabatta. Halve each sandwich on the diagonal and serve.

SPICY RED RUB

Makes about ¾ cup

Use this rub whenever you want to add a little kick to something. It works great on vegetables and meat alike.

3 tablespoons smoked paprika

3 tablespoons cumin seeds, toasted and ground

2 tablespoons kosher salt

2 tablespoons sugar

1½ tablespoons whole cloves, toasted and ground

1 tablespoon cayenne

1 tablespoon mustard seeds, toasted and ground

Combine all of the ingredients in a jar with a tight-fitting lid. Stir with a spoon to thoroughly mix. The rub will keep, tightly covered, for up to 3 months.

Serves 4

Roast four salmon fillets and sauté some spinach, it's as simple—and almost as quick—as that. The salmon on its bed of spinach is also beautiful when served family style on a large platter.

4 (5-ounce) salmon fillets, skin on
Kosher salt
Fresh ground black pepper
¼ cup Spicy Red Rub (page 55)
4 teaspoons extra virgin olive oil
2 cloves garlic, thinly sliced
8 cups packed baby spinach (one 16-ounce bag)
½ cup Chipotle Yogurt Sauce (page 51)
16 Roasted Cherry Tomatoes (page 114) with their juices

Preheat the oven to 400°F. Season each of the fillets with salt and pepper. Dredge in spice rub and shake off the excess.

Heat 2 teaspoons of the olive oil in a large skillet over medium heat. Place the fillets in the skillet, skin side down, and pan roast for 1 minute. Turn the fillets and cook for 1 minute longer.

Transfer the fillets to the baking sheet, skin side down, and roast in the oven until the fish is opaque at the center, about 6 minutes (rare) to 8 minutes (medium).

Meanwhile, wipe out the skillet with paper towels. Add the remaining 2 teaspoons olive oil and the garlic to the pan. Place over medium heat. Sauté until the garlic is fragrant and soft, add the spinach, season with salt and pepper, and sauté until the spinach wilts.

To plate, spoon about 2 tablespoons chipotle sauce onto each dinner plate. Arrange the spinach over. Add the tomatoes to the skillet and immediately remove from the heat just to warm them. Arrange the fillets over the spinach, then divide the tomatoes among each plate.

NOTE: I serve this family-style on a larger platter placed in the middle of our table. This is the way we eat at home—simple, not fussy, and good.

GARDEN VEGETABLES AND FRUITS

GARDEN VEGETABLES AND FRUITS

HERE'S HOW SUNDAY AFTERNOONS GO IN OUR HOUSE: I PUT A BIG POT of water on to boil, dump ice in a large bowl and fill it with water, trim cauliflower, broccoli, haricots verts (French green beans), and any other vegetables we might want during the week, and let the blanching and shocking begin. Next comes the fruit. Depending on what's in season—lots of citrus in the winter and watermelon all summer long—I prep them so that during the week, there's nothing more to do than reach into the refrigerator for a snack or quick salad.

This has become a weekend ritual and a huge time saver for my wife, who does the cooking during the week. The payoff is enormous. It takes little more than 90 minutes to prepare for the week—which is minimal when you consider just how little time and effort it will take to make dinner on the weeknights. Most recipes in this chapter take no more than 20 minutes to pull together when you have blanched vegetables on hand.

In my house, we are so much more likely to eat our vegetables and fruits if we have them ready for quick cooking and eating. When my kids come home from school, they snack on blanched and shocked cauliflower with Garlic Yogurt Sauce (page 31). On those all-too-typical nights when we are rushing to get dinner on the table, there's nothing like reaching into the fridge and tossing broccoli into the pan at the last minute, just to warm it through. That broccoli is a gift. No chopping, no steaming, no draining—and fewer dishes to clean up. And by just adding crumbled feta and mint to a mix of citrus fruit—all segmented over the weekend—we can have a fresh, healthful dinner salad on the table in minutes.

If you want to eat well, it's essential to keep fresh vegetables and fruits in your fridge at all times. I am also a big proponent of putting them on the kids' plates whether they like them or not. One of my strategies is to tuck all the good stuff I can into the dishes I know they love. Like so many young kids, their ardor for rice and pasta is unparalleled. I toss cauliflower in and they barely notice. One of my favorite recipes here is Cinnamon-Scented Cauliflower in Tomato Sauce (page 71), which I have to credit for putting me on the Live to Eat path. It is one of the few recipes in this book that I've taken straight from my Greek heritage because it can't be improved upon—unless you add raisins, olives, and pine nuts, as I do in the variation. It is a good example of building on a basic recipe to create layers of flavor—a key component of the Live to Eat way of cooking and eating. That same Cinnamon-Scented Cauliflower becomes a soup (page 72) simply by adding water to the intensely flavored tomato base.

Preparing most vegetables isn't rocket science, but there's a particular technique I use that is ideal for making quick, flavorful side dishes. Before adding vegetables to a pan, I heat oil and infuse it with garlic and pepperoncini. This creates an intense layer of flavor to the vegetables without adding much fat or any other unhealthy ingredients. Think of it this way: Infused olive oil plus any blanched and shocked vegetable plus any crushed nut equals an excellent side dish!

Of course, I draw on my Greek heritage heavily when it comes to cooking vegetables, but I have modernized some classic recipes for the Live to Eat diet. For example, my mother always stewed string beans to the point where they almost disintegrated, but I like the texture of the warm blanched haricots verts and the flavor of fresh, juicy tomatoes in my Haricots Verts with Tomatoes and Feta (page 77). To that end, I skip all that stewing and toss all of the ingredients together in my Red Wine Vinaigrette (page 192) to keep things bright and textured.

If you have only one blanched vegetable in your refrigerator, make it broccoli. There are recipes here that I hope will make using it reflexive: Warm it and toss with olive oil, fresh lemon juice, and salt or grill it to give it a nice smoky flavor. Or, toss it into pasta or an omelet or a frittata. Or dress it in garlic and pepperoncini infused olive oil. Or...

BLANCHED AND SHOCKED VEGETABLES

Blanching and shocking is nothing more than plunging vegetables into boiling, salted water to cook them until they are still firm, yet soft enough to bite into, then plunging them into an ice water bath to halt the cooking process. Simply drain and store in a container in the fridge to pull out at a moment's notice. The beauty of blanching is that you can use the same boiling water for all vegetables; just be sure to begin with cauliflower and move on to the haricots verts and broccoli to prevent the white florets from taking on a green tinge. One bonus is that the leftover cooking water makes a light vegetable stock that you can use in soups, to thin sauces, and deglaze pans.

Blanching is simple and the best results come if you use a pot big enough to allow the vegetables to move around freely. Also, be sure to liberally salt the water. I don't give amounts here; I leave it to you to blanch as much as you think you may need for the week (but don't forget to add enough to snack on). Leftovers are a gift: You can chop and toss any and all of these into an omelet, throw into a pot with some stock and whir into a soup (add Greek yogurt and fresh soft herbs), or toss with pasta.

Bring a large pot of salted water to a boil. Prepare an ice bath in a large bowl. Line a baking sheet with paper towels.

Meanwhile, prepare the vegetables:

Cauliflower: Remove the green leaves from the cauliflower and discard. Cut the head in half lengthwise and cut out the solid stem and core entirely. Break into big florets by hand. Using a knife, trim the larger pieces into ½- to 1-inch pieces (or a size that is comfortable to put in your mouth). Cut the stalks into ⅛-inch-thick slices.

Broccoli: Remove the green leaves from the broccoli and discard. Cut away the tough portion of the stem and discard. Using a knife, separate the florets into ½- to 1-inch pieces (or a size that is comfortable to put in your mouth). Cut the stalks into ⅛-inch-thick slices.

Haricots verts: Trim the stem ends.

Broccoli rabe: Cut stalks with leaves into ½-inch pieces on the diagonal and cut florets off the stalk whole.

Blanch the vegetables—Working in batches so that the water continues to boil, dump the vegetables, one type at a time, working from lightest to darkest, into the boiling water. Cook, checking every 30 seconds, until a knife pierces the vegetable with a little effort. You don't want them cooked all the way through because you will be reheating them. To test, use a slotted spoon to remove one vegetable and dip into the ice water. Taste for doneness. The vegetable should be firm to the bite and look vibrant.

Shock the vegetables—Using a slotted spoon, transfer the vegetables to the ice water to stop the cooking process (and to preserve the boiling water, which is now a light stock). Let sit until they are cool. Transfer the vegetables to the paper towel–lined sheet to dry. Let the cooking water cool and transfer to rigid containers to use as a vegetable stock. It will keep for up to 1 week in the refrigerator or 1 month in the freezer.

Dry the vegetables—Pat the vegetables all over to ensure they are completely dry; water on vegetables is the devil and will cause them to deteriorate quickly. Line a rigid storage container with paper towels and transfer the vegetables to it. Each time you use the vegetable, replace the paper towel to combat condensation, which is inevitable if the container sits on the counter and then goes back into the refrigerator.

CAULIFLOWER

GARLICKY CAULIFLOWER WITH ENGLISH PEAS AND MINT

Serves 4

So simple, so good. One of my faves. It is a healthy snack—at room temperature—or a light vegetarian lunch with a green salad. It also goes with chicken, fish, and beef.

¼ cup canola oil
1 head cauliflower, cut into florets (about 4 cups), blanched and shocked (see page 62)
¼ cup extra virgin olive oil
8 cloves garlic, thinly sliced
¼ teaspoon chile flakes, optional
Kosher salt
Fresh ground black pepper
1½ cups English peas, thawed if frozen
8 mint leaves, rough chopped
Juice of 1 lemon
6 tablespoons Garlic Puree (page 141)

Heat the canola oil in a large skillet over medium heat. Add the cauliflower and sear the florets, turning occasionally, until they are golden in places. Add the olive oil along with the garlic and chile flakes, if using, and season with salt and pepper. Sauté until the garlic is golden and fragrant. Add the peas and mint and toss to coat with the oil. Sauté for a few seconds, just until the mint is fragrant. Add the lemon juice and ½ cup water and cook until the liquid is slightly reduced. Stir in the garlic puree and cook, tossing, just until the vegetables are coated. Serve warm.

VARIATION: WITH ROASTED SALMON

High-heat roasting allows you to sear the outside of salmon and quickly develop an amazingly crispy crust. Thoroughly pat dry four 5-ounce salmon fillets, season with salt and pepper, place skin side down in a roasting pan slicked with canola oil, and roast in a 500°F oven for 10 minutes. Divide the cauliflower among four dinner plates and arrange a fillet over it. Drizzle some **Ladolemono** (page 161) over the fish and serve warm.

PENNE WITH CAULIFLOWER, PEAS, AND PEPPERONCINI

Serves 4

Just ½ cup of pasta per person may seem stingy, but plentiful vegetables make this dish completely satisfying. You'll see my love for garlic here—12 cloves may seem like a lot, but it provides just the right amount of zing.

6 ounces (2 cups) dry whole wheat penne or any other short pasta
¼ cup canola oil
2 heads cauliflower, cut into florets (about 8 cups), blanched and shocked (see page 62)
¼ cup extra virgin olive oil
12 cloves garlic, thinly sliced
4 pepperoncini, thinly sliced into rings
Pinch chile flakes
Kosher salt
Fresh ground black pepper
Juice of 1 lemon
3 cups English peas, thawed if frozen
¾ **cup Garlic Puree (page 141)**

Cook the pasta according to package directions and drain.

Meanwhile, heat the canola oil in a large skillet over medium heat. Add the cauliflower and sear the florets, turning occasionally, until they are golden in places. Add the olive oil along with the sliced garlic, pepperoncini, and chile flakes and season with salt and pepper. Sauté until the garlic is golden and fragrant. Add the lemon juice, peas, and 1 cup water to the skillet and cook, scraping up any bits on the bottom of the pan, until the liquid is reduced by half. Stir in the garlic puree and cook until it is warmed through.

Add the pasta to the pan and cook until there is no liquid left in the pan and the sauce clings to the pasta—it will take just a minute. Serve warm.

EGG WHITE FRITTATA
WITH SPINACH, CAULIFLOWER, AND FETA

Serves 4

Frittatas are open to all manner of toss-ins—we often use whatever blanched vegetables, cheeses, and herbs happen to be in the refrigerator. Breakfast, lunch, or dinner—this crustless egg "pie" is a healthy option any time of day. I love it tucked into a ciabatta sandwich loaf for lunch.

Extra virgin olive oil to coat the skillet
1 head cauliflower, cut into florets (about 4 cups), blanched and shocked (see page 62), and broken into ½-inch pieces
4 cloves garlic, thinly sliced
4 cups loosely packed chopped spinach
8 large mint leaves, chopped
Kosher salt
Fresh ground black pepper
16 large egg whites (2 cups), beaten until foamy
½ cup crumbled feta cheese

Preheat the oven to 500°F.

Heat a large cast-iron skillet slicked with olive oil over medium heat. Add the cauliflower and sear, turning occasionally, until golden in places. Add the garlic and sauté until golden and fragrant. Add the spinach and cook, tossing, until the spinach wilts. Add the mint and toss to evenly distribute. Season with salt and pepper.

Spread the mixture evenly in the pan, then pour the egg whites over. Scatter the feta over the eggs. Transfer to the oven and bake until the egg whites are set; they shouldn't jiggle when you shake the pan, 10 to 12 minutes. Serve in cast iron skillet to keep warm.

PAN-ROASTED SCALLOPS WITH
WARM CINNAMON-CAULIFLOWER SALAD

Serves 4

Prepare this once, and it will become a weekly staple. It has everything going for it: It's healthy, delicious, easy—and only requires one skillet! You can use peeled and deveined shrimp in place of the scallops if you like.

2 tablespoons extra virgin olive oil
8 dry diver scallops (see headnote, page 126), patted completely dry
Kosher salt
Fresh ground black pepper
3 cups cauliflower florets, blanched and shocked (see page 62)
Pinch ground cinnamon
2 tablespoons butter
1 small shallot, finely chopped
1 tablespoon capers, rinsed and drained
4 sage leaves, thinly sliced
4 cups loosely packed chopped spinach
2 tablespoons tart dried cherries
Ladolemono (page 161) for drizzling

Heat 1 tablespoon of the olive oil in a large skillet over medium heat. Season the scallops with salt and pepper. Add the scallops to the pan and sear on both sides, resisting the temptation to move them around before they develop a good sear. Transfer the scallops to a plate and wipe out the skillet.

Add the remaining 1 tablespoon oil to the pan and return to the heat. Add the cauliflower, sprinkle with the cinnamon, and sauté until the cauliflower is browned in spots. Add the butter to the pan along with the shallot, capers, and sage and sauté until the shallots are soft and golden. Add the spinach and cherries and sauté until the spinach wilts. Season with salt and pepper.

Divide the cauliflower mixture among four plates and arrange two scallops over each. Drizzle with a little ladolemono and serve warm.

NOTE: You may substitute 2 teaspoons of extra virgin olive oil for butter if you don't want to cheat.

ISRAELI COUSCOUS WITH SHRIMP, CAULIFLOWER, PEAS, AND MINT

Serves 4

A good Greek would use orzo here, but I love the toothiness you get by using whole grain Israeli couscous instead. It is considered children's food in Israel, but the adults in my house are just as fond of it.

1 cup whole grain dry Israeli couscous
¼ cup canola oil
1½ heads cauliflower, cut into florets (about 6 cups), blanched and shocked (see page 62)
¼ cup olive oil
10 cloves garlic, thinly sliced
20 large shrimp (15/20 per pound), peeled, deveined, tails removed, halved lengthwise
3 cups English peas, thawed if frozen
¾ cup Garlic Puree (page 141)
12 mint leaves
Juice of 1 lemon
Kosher salt
Fresh ground black pepper

Prepare the couscous according to package directions.

Heat the canola oil in a large skillet over medium heat. Add the cauliflower and sear the florets, turning occasionally, until golden in spots, resisting the urge to move them until the parts touching the pan are properly seared. Add the olive oil and garlic and sauté until golden and fragrant. Add the couscous, 2 cups water, the shrimp, peas, garlic puree, mint, and lemon juice and season with salt and pepper. Cook until the shrimp are opaque, the water has completely evaporated, and the pan is dry. Serve warm.

NOTE: Substitute farro, freekah, wheatberry, or any other whole grain for an even healthier version with a little more crunch.

CINNAMON-SCENTED CAULIFLOWER IN TOMATO SAUCE

Serves 4

Serve this as a side dish with roasted meats and poultry, or spoon it over brown rice or a little pasta for a vegetarian main course. The truth is, it's delicious straight out of the fridge as a snack.

¼ cup canola oil
½ medium yellow onion, cut into slivers
1 head cauliflower, cut into florets (about 4 cups), blanched and shocked (see page 62)
4 cloves garlic, thinly sliced
Pinch of cinnamon
2 cups Tomato Sauce (page 174)
Kosher salt
Fresh ground black pepper

Heat the oil in a large skillet over medium heat. Add the onion and sauté until soft and translucent. Add the cauliflower and garlic and sprinkle the cinnamon over. Sauté until the garlic is golden and fragrant. Add the tomato sauce and 1½ cups water. Season with salt and pepper. Cook until the cauliflower soaks up all of the sauce. Serve warm.

VARIATION: WITH OLIVES, RAISINS, AND PINE NUTS

Prepare the recipe as directed, and as the sauce is reducing in the last step, add 20 Greek olives, ½ cup golden raisins, ¼ cup toasted pine nuts or crushed smoked almonds, and **2 tablespoons Garlic Puree (page 141).** Season with salt and black pepper and stir to thoroughly incorporate. Serve warm.

VARIATION: WITH WHOLE WHEAT RIGATONI, OLIVES, RAISINS, AND PINE NUTS

Make this a main course by doubling the variation recipe and adding 6 ounces of cooked whole wheat rigatoni to the pan right after stirring in the olives, raisins, pine nuts, and garlic puree. Cook the pasta and sauce until the sauce reduces and clings to the pasta. Drizzle a bit of extra virgin olive oil over and serve.

CINNAMON-SCENTED CAULIFLOWER AND TOMATO SOUP

Serves 4

If you have shocked and blanched cauliflower on hand, this soup can be ready in a few minutes. Taste and adjust the amount of vinegar it needs as you go.

¼ cup canola oil
½ medium yellow onion, cut into slivers
1 head cauliflower, cut into florets (about 4 cups), blanched and shocked (see page 62)
4 cloves garlic, thinly sliced
Pinch of cinnamon
2 cups Tomato Sauce (page 174)
Kosher salt
Fresh ground black pepper
Red wine vinegar

Heat the oil in a large pot over medium heat. Add the onion and sauté until soft and translucent. Add the cauliflower and garlic and sprinkle the cinnamon over. Sauté until the garlic is golden and fragrant. Add the tomato sauce and 3 cups water. Season with salt and pepper and cook until the liquid is gurgling and thoroughly warmed through. Add vinegar to taste and season with salt and pepper. Serve hot.

RIGATONI WITH CHICKEN AND TOMATO-STEWED CAULIFLOWER

Serves 4

Chicken tenderloins are not often called for in pasta dishes, but I love using them because they cook quickly and stay tender and moist. The cauliflower here is deeply flavorful; you can leave the chicken out of the dish entirely to make it vegetarian.

6 ounces uncooked whole wheat rigatoni or other short pasta

¼ cup canola oil

1½ heads cauliflower, cut into florets (about 6 cups), blanched and shocked (see page 62)

¼ cup extra virgin olive oil, plus more for drizzling

8 cloves garlic, thinly sliced

4 pepperoncini, seeds removed, chopped

¼ teaspoon chile flakes

Kosher salt

Fresh ground black pepper

3 cups Tomato Sauce (page 174)

¼ cup Garlic Puree (page 141)

8 chicken tenderloins, cut into ¼-inch pieces

¼ cup chopped fresh dill

¼ cup grated pecorino cheese

Cook the pasta according to package instructions.

Heat the canola oil in a large skillet over medium heat. Add the cauliflower and sear until the florets are golden in places. Add the olive oil, sliced garlic, pepperoncini, and chile flakes and season with salt and pepper. Sauté until the garlic is golden and fragrant. Add the tomato sauce, 3 cups water, and the garlic puree and stir. Cook until the liquid is reduced by half.

Add the cooked pasta, chicken, and dill and leave on the heat until the chicken is cooked through and the sauce clings to the pasta, about 2 minutes. Drizzle olive oil over and garnish with the pecorino. Serve warm.

NOTE: Don't forget to salt the water before cooking pasta!

GARDEN VEGETABLES AND FRUITS

HARICOTS VERTS

WITH HARICOTS VERTS IN YOUR REFRIGERATOR, YOU CAN MAKE:
Pickled Beet Salad (page 35)
Sautéed Haricots Verts with Pepperoncini and Smoked Almonds (below)
Haricots Verts with Tomatoes and Feta (page 77)
Sautéed Haricots Verts with Slivered Red Onions (page 77)
Niçoise Salad, Greek Style (page 207)

SAUTÉED HARICOTS VERTS WITH PEPPERONCINI AND SMOKED ALMONDS

Serves 4

The key here is to flavor the oil with the garlic and pepperoncini *before* tossing the beans in. Make sure to add the chile flakes at the same time you toss in the beans; any earlier and the flakes will burn.

6 tablespoons extra virgin olive oil
4 cloves garlic, thinly sliced
4 pepperoncini, seeds removed, thinly sliced into rings
¼ teaspoon chile flakes
1 pound haricots verts or green beans, blanched and shocked (see page 62)
Kosher salt
Fresh ground black pepper
¼ cup crushed smoked almonds (optional)

Combine the olive oil, garlic, and pepperoncini in a large skillet over medium heat. Sauté until the garlic is golden and fragrant. As the garlic begins to take on color, add the chile flakes and beans. Season with salt and pepper. Sauté, tossing occasionally, until the beans brighten in color. Transfer the beans to a platter and garnish with the almonds. Serve warm.

Serves 4

This is a great go-to summer salad, when tomatoes are at their peak. Of course, you can substitute any blanched vegetable for the green beans.

28 haricots verts or green beans, blanched and shocked (see page 62)

4 medium heirloom tomatoes, cut into 1-inch pieces (see page 12)

36 oil-cured olives, pitted

½ red onion, cut into ¼-inch-thick slices

¼ teaspoon dried oregano

Kosher salt

Fresh ground black pepper

2 tablespoons Red Wine Vinaigrette (page 192)

1 tablespoon extra virgin olive oil

2 tablespoons crumbled feta cheese

Combine the beans, tomatoes, olives, onion, oregano, and salt and pepper to taste in a large bowl. Add the vinaigrette and olive oil and toss to thoroughly coat. Transfer to a platter and scatter the feta over. Serve at room temperature.

SAUTÉED HARICOTS VERTS WITH SLIVERED RED ONIONS

Serves 4

This is a simple dish. Be sure to sauté the garlic until it just starts to turn golden brown so that the oil is fully infused with its mellow flavor.

½ cup extra virgin olive oil, plus more for drizzling

1 medium red onion, cut into slivers

4 cloves garlic, thinly sliced

1 pound haricots verts or green beans, blanched and shocked (see page 62)

Kosher salt

Fresh ground black pepper

8 teaspoons red wine vinegar

Combine half of the olive oil, the onion, and garlic in a large skillet over medium heat. Sauté until fragrant and the onions are slightly softened. Add beans, toss, and season with salt and pepper. Add remaining olive oil, half of the vinegar, and 1 teaspoon water. Toss to coat the beans and heat through. Transfer to a platter and drizzle with the remaining vinegar. Serve warm.

BROCCOLI

WITH BROCCOLI OR BROCCOLI RABE IN YOUR REFRIGERATOR, YOU CAN MAKE:

Simple Steamed Broccoli with Lemon and Olive Oil (below)

Broccoli with Crispy Garlic (page 80)

Egg White Frittata with Broccoli, Spinach, and Feta (page 81)

Grilled Broccoli with Lemon and Olive Oil (page 83)

Spicy Mediterranean Shrimp Stir-Fry (page 101)

Spicy Shrimp with Cauliflower and Broccoli in Garlic Sauce (page 152)

Chicken with Broccoli, Peas, and Artichokes (page 158)

Rigatoni with Chicken Sausage and Broccoli Rabe (page 159)

Sautéed Pork Tenderloin with Spicy Tomato-Braised Broccoli Rabe (page 182)

SIMPLE STEAMED BROCCOLI WITH LEMON AND OLIVE OIL

Serves 4

Olive oil, salt, and lemon: If there are three ingredients that can transform a vegetable, these are the ones. In fact, if a savory dish is lacking, this trio can brighten and intensify the flavors instantly. Use the best-quality olive oil you can get your hands on and use the combo with abandon.

Juice of 1 lemon, plus some wedges
  for serving

¼ cup extra virgin olive oil

**6 cups broccoli florets, blanched and
  shocked (see page 62)**

Kosher salt

Fresh ground black pepper

Squeeze the lemon juice into a medium bowl, then add the olive oil. Warm the broccoli in the microwave. Transfer to the bowl and toss to coat. Season with salt and pepper, transfer to a platter, and serve with the lemon wedges.

BROCCOLI WITH CRISPY GARLIC

Serves 4

Crisped garlic is addictive—and a healthy way to get the salty crunch you might seek from, say, potato chips—which is why you should incorporate it into as many dishes as you can. Here, I toss it with broccoli and pepperoncini, but use your imagination: It is hard to go wrong using it with any vegetable.

6 cups broccoli florets, blanched and shocked (see page 62)
½ cup extra virgin olive oil
4 cloves garlic, thinly sliced
4 pepperoncini, seeds removed, thinly sliced into rings
Kosher salt
Fresh ground black pepper
Pinch chile flakes
Juice of 1 lemon

Warm the broccoli in the microwave and transfer to a platter.

Heat the olive oil in a large skillet over medium heat. Add the garlic and pepperoncini and season with salt and pepper.

As the garlic browns, add the chile flakes and sauté until fragrant, about 10 seconds. Pour over the broccoli, finish with a squeeze of lemon juice, and serve warm.

EGG WHITE FRITTATA WITH BROCCOLI, SPINACH, AND FETA

Serves 4

You will not miss the egg yolks one bit in this deeply flavorful take on the classic egg dish. It's my wife's favorite thing to eat—for breakfast, lunch, or dinner.

4 cloves garlic, thinly sliced
¼ cup canola oil
4 cups broccoli florets, blanched and shocked (see page 62)
2 cups packed spinach, chopped
Kosher salt
Fresh ground black pepper
16 egg whites (2 cups), beaten until foamy
½ cup crumbled feta cheese

Preheat the oven to 500°F.

Sauté the garlic in the oil in a large oven-proof skillet over medium heat until golden. Add the broccoli and spinach, season with salt and pepper, and cook just until the spinach wilts. Pour the egg whites over and sprinkle the feta on top. Transfer to the oven and bake until the egg whites are set, 10 to 12 minutes; they shouldn't jiggle when you shake the pan. Let cool until the eggs are fully set. Cut the frittata into wedges and serve warm.

GRILLED BROCCOLI WITH LEMON AND OLIVE OIL

Serves 4

Grilling broccoli changes its flavor dramatically—it becomes smoky, crisp, and tender at the same time. If you are going to fire up the grill for this, why not grill some cauliflower or other blanched vegetables and a few pounded chicken breasts for later use?

¼ cup Ladolemono (page 161)
Juice of 1 lemon
6 cups broccoli florets, blanched and shocked (see page 62)
½ cup extra virgin olive oil, plus more for drizzling
Kosher salt
Fresh ground black pepper

Preheat a gas grill or grill pan over medium heat. Combine the ladolemono and lemon juice in a large bowl and set aside. Toss the broccoli in the olive oil to coat and season with salt and pepper.

Working in batches if necessary, place the florets in a grilling basket to prevent them from falling through the grate and grill until charred, turning once or twice. Transfer to the bowl with the ladolemono and toss to coat. Transfer to a serving platter, drizzle with a little olive oil, and serve.

NOTE: Any leftover grilled broccoli is shockingly good in a simple pasta with browned garlic. Add any leftover chicken if you want some protein. I love a sprinkle of chile flakes for a touch of heat.

I think watermelon sometimes scares people because a whole one just takes up too much room in the fridge. Luckily you can buy one that is precut and makes sense for your family. I always cut it into pieces immediately so we can all snack on it whenever. Up to you whether you leave the rind on or not. Truth is, I don't know if there is a better summertime treat.

GRILLED WATERMELON WITH FETA

Serves 4

Grilling adds another dimension to this traditional dish—you can skip it altogether but the heat lends a fourth "flavor" to the sweet, salty, sour combination. Serve with any grilled meat, poultry, or fish.

¼ watermelon, rind removed and cut into 16 (¾-inch-thick) wedges
Olive oil
Kosher salt
Fresh ground black pepper
1 cup crumbled feta cheese
2 teaspoons honey, optional
8 mint leaves, snipped with scissors

Preheat a gas grill or grill pan over medium heat. Rub one side of each piece of watermelon with olive oil. Season with salt and pepper. Arrange the oiled side of the watermelon on the grill and grill for 30 seconds—just long enough to impart the flavor of the grill. Transfer the fruit to a platter and scatter the feta over. Drizzle with more olive oil and honey, if desired. Season with salt and pepper and scatter the mint over. Serve warm.

NOTE: Be careful not to overcook the watermelon. The goal is to add a smoky char for depth of flavor. The watermelon should still stay crunchy and cool.

ARUGULA WITH WATERMELON, RED ONION, AND FETA

Serves 4 to 6

A green, a fruit, an onion, and a cheese—this is my summer version of an ideal salad, but you can just as easily substitute seasonal fruit for winter, spring, and fall. Watermelon and onions may seem an unusual pair, but the mingling of sweet and heat allows your mouth to alternately cool down and warm up.

4 cups loosely packed arugula
½ medium onion, cut into slivers
12 mint leaves, snipped with scissors into coarse pieces, plus a few tiny leaves left whole
2 tablespoons Red Wine Vinaigrette (page 192)
Kosher salt
Fresh ground black pepper
¼ watermelon, rind removed and cut into 8 (½-inch-thick) triangles
½ cup crumbled feta cheese
Extra virgin olive oil for drizzling

Toss the arugula, onion, and mint with the vinaigrette to thoroughly coat. Season with salt and pepper. Arrange the watermelon on a platter and scatter half of the feta over it. Arrange the greens over and scatter the remaining feta on the greens. Drizzle a bit of olive oil around the platter, season with a pinch of pepper. Garnish with the mint and serve.

VARIATION: The addition of rare seared tuna to this salad makes for a complete meal. Preheat a pan with a slick of canola oil on medium-high heat. Season the tuna on both sides with salt and pepper. Sear for two minutes on each side. Slice against the grain about ¼ inch thick and toss with salad.

Any dish made with citrus is only as good as the fruit you select. Of course, oranges, lemons, and limes are available throughout the year, but you'll notice that the best show up in the market in the winter months. Of the several types of oranges available, my favorite is Cara Cara, a red-fleshed navel that is wonderfully sweet. If given a choice, I pick key limes over the Persian variety, for their combination of bitter and sweet flavor as well as their wonderful aroma. As far as lemons go, I love the sweetness of deep yellow Meyers; they play well with oranges.

Throughout, I ask you to segment citrus, which simply means you remove the peel and white pith and then excise the fruit from its membrane (see Sectioning Citrus, page 12).

WITH CITRUS IN YOUR REFRIGERATOR, YOU CAN MAKE:

Pickled Beet Salad (page 35)

Fluke Sushi with Orange and Mint (below)

Citrus Salad with Greek Yogurt (page 89)

Citrus Salad with Feta and Mint (page 89)

Spicy Pork Sofrito with Fennel, Oranges, and Olives (page 155)

Shaved Fennel, Red Onion, and Grapefruit Salad (page 205)

FLUKE SUSHI WITH ORANGE AND MINT

Makes 20 pieces / Serves 4

This combination tastes great with any white, flaky, sushi-grade fish, which really acts as a textural platform for the orange and mint. Yellowtail is a nice alternative.

1¼ cups Brown Sushi Rice (page 41)

4 ounces fluke or yellowtail, sliced against the grain on an angle into 20 (½- x 1½-inch) slices

Extra virgin olive oil for rubbing

4 orange segments, each cut into 5 very thin slices

1 small lemon, halved

Sea salt

Fresh ground black pepper

4 mint leaves, cut into thin strips

20 thinly sliced rings jalapeño pepper

Wet your hands and scoop 1 tablespoon of the rice into one palm. Make a fist around it to shape into a ½- x 1-inch rectangle. Push the ends in with your thumb and index finger to create clean edges. Put the rice block on a platter and repeat with the remaining rice.

Drape a slice of fluke over each rectangle, then rub each with olive oil. Top each with an orange slice and a drop of lemon juice. Season with salt and pepper. Top with a mint strip and a ring of jalapeño. Serve immediately.

CITRUS SALAD WITH GREEK YOGURT

Serves 4

I like to think of this as a healthy sundae, one that even kids will love.

**1 ruby red grapefruit,
segmented with its juices**
**1 Cara Cara or other navel orange,
segmented with its juices**
1 key lime, segmented with its juices
16 ounces Greek yogurt
Sea salt
Fresh ground black pepper
1 tablespoon honey
8 mint leaves, roughly chopped

Combine the grapefruit, orange, and lime segments and their juices in a bowl. Spoon the yogurt into each of four dessert bowls. Divide the citrus mixture and juice among them and season with salt and pepper. Drizzle the honey over and garnish with the mint.

NOTE: Basil also works here.

CITRUS SALAD WITH FETA AND MINT

Serves 4 to 6

Think of the fruit here as suggestions—use any mix you like.

**2 ruby red grapefruits, segmented
with their juices**
**4 Cara Cara or other navel oranges,
segmented with their juices**
**2 key limes, segmented with their
juices**
2 teaspoons extra virgin olive oil
Juice of 1 lemon
Kosher salt
Fresh ground black pepper
1 tablespoon crumbled feta cheese
8 mint leaves, rough chop

Combine the grapefruit, orange, and lime segments with their juices in a bowl. Dress with the olive oil and lemon juice. Season with salt and pepper and toss. Sprinkle the feta and mint over and refrigerate for 10 minutes. Serve cold.

SWEET AND SOUR
PEPPERS AND ONIONS

SWEET AND SOUR PEPPERS AND ONIONS

PEPPERS AND ONIONS: ALMOST EVERY CULTURE'S CUISINE HAS DEVELOPED a version of this humble combination. Perhaps they are so common together because they can transform almost any dish.

My secret is to turn them into a sweet and sour mixture. The obvious use is as a condiment for grilled meats, chicken, and fish. One of my favorite techniques that incorporates onions and peppers is to sear a piece of chicken, pork, or steak on both sides, remove it from the pan, add a liquid (water, wine, stock) to deglaze and scrape up all the good bits, then add the pepper and onions and heat through. It's a template for making a quick dinner and the technique becomes reflexive after doing it a few times. But you can also thin the mixture a bit with water and wine and add some olives and garlic to make a Mediterranean Salsa (page 104). Or add cilantro and feta cheese to create a Mediterranean-style sauce. Once I developed the master recipe, I couldn't stop adding variations. I even added chunky bits of celery, olives, and almonds and some herbs to make my favorite dip (page 96).

The dishes I created to go with peppers and onions are so varied they surprised even me. There's a shrimp stir-fry, sushi, pasta, tacos, a couple chicken dishes, salsa, and eggs. In devising the recipes, I tapped into Italian, Asian, American, Mexican, and Middle Eastern influences, each one employing the use of peppers and onions through their distinctive culinary lenses.

So, if onions and peppers are a panacea, there must be a catch, right? They do take time to make—at least an hour. However, their flavor develops over time in the fridge and they're best if prepared in advance. Remember, time often equals flavor, so having these on hand is an essential shortcut to putting quick but terrific dinners on the table during the week.

Prepare this on the weekend and chose three meals to make with them over the course of the week. It's a culinary chameleon, a cook's secret weapon. Take the time to prepare it. It's worth it.

WITH SWEET AND SOUR PEPPERS AND ONIONS IN YOUR REFRIGERATOR, YOU CAN MAKE:

SWEET AND SOUR PEPPERS AND ONIONS

Makes 10 cups

This basic recipe, made sour with vinegar and sweet with honey, is quite malleable—so add your favorite ingredients to flavor it: Chile flakes add heat, crushed toasted nuts add texture and depth, chopped fresh herbs brighten it.

This makes far more than you will need for any one recipe, but you can freeze what you don't use in 1-cup portions in rigid freezer-safe containers with tight-fitting lids or in resealable plastic bags. Thaw at room temperature or defrost in the microwave before using.

¼ cup canola oil

4 yellow bell peppers, cut lengthwise into ¼-inch-thick strips

4 red bell peppers, cut lengthwise into ¼-inch-thick strips

3 large yellow onions, cut into slivers

15 cloves garlic, roughly chopped

6 tablespoons tomato paste

1 cup white wine vinegar

½ cup dry white wine

2 cups Tomato Sauce (page 174)

2 tablespoons honey

2 tablespoons kosher salt

½ teaspoon fresh ground black pepper

In a large heavy-bottomed pot over medium-high heat, combine the canola oil and peppers and sauté until just softened and fragrant and the peppers begin to release a little liquid, 5 to 8 minutes. Add the onions and garlic and sauté just until the onions are soft; do not let them take on any color. Add the tomato paste and stir to combine. Add the vinegar and white wine and cook until the liquid is reduced by half. (The larger the pan, the faster the liquid in the mixture will reduce.)

Add 6 cups water, the tomato sauce, honey, salt, and pepper and stir. Bring the mixture to a boil, then reduce the heat and simmer until the liquid thickens to the consistency of a salsa. The peppers and onions will keep, tightly covered, in the refrigerator for 1 week, or for up to 3 months in the freezer.

PASTA WITH SAUSAGE AND PEPPERS

Serves 4

Here's the classic dish, revamped a bit to use chicken sausage instead of pork, which can be fattier. It is every bit as lusty and satisfying as its richer counterpart, thanks to the generous addition of mellow, creamy garlic puree, an ingredient I'm not sure I could live without.

3 cups short whole wheat pasta, such as rigatoni

¼ cup plus 4 teaspoons extra virgin olive oil

8 cloves garlic, thinly sliced

4 cups Sweet and Sour Peppers and Onions (page 94)

14 ounces chicken sausages, cut into ½-inch pieces

¼ cup Garlic Puree (page 141)

Kosher salt

Fresh ground black pepper

20 large basil leaves, roughly chopped

4 teaspoons grated pecorino cheese

4 teaspoons crumbled feta cheese

Cook the pasta according to package directions and drain.

Heat ¼ cup of the olive oil and the sliced garlic in a large saucepan over medium heat and sauté until soft and golden. Add 2 cups water, the peppers and onions, and sausage and cook until the sausage is no longer pink and the liquid has thickened, about 8 minutes.

Just before the sauce is thickened, stir in the garlic puree, then add the cooked pasta and toss. Cook until the sauce clings to the pasta. Season with salt and pepper. Drizzle the remaining olive oil over, add the basil, and toss. Transfer to a serving bowl. Sprinkle with the pecorino and feta, season to taste, and serve warm.

Tip: Whenever I make pasta I cook a little more than I need and set it aside. I always seem to find a use for it sometime during the week.

SWEET AND SOUR PEPPERS AND ONIONS

MY FAVORITE VEGETABLE DIP

Makes about 2 cups / Serves 4

Like the Garlic Yogurt Sauce (page 31), this is a fantastic dip on its own with vegetables and pita, but it is also a key ingredient in Bulgur Salad (page 108). I even love it as a condiment with grilled meat and chicken. Double the recipe so that you can have it both ways: Enjoy as a dip and have enough on hand to make the salad on another day. The thinner you slice the olives, the more their flavor will permeate the dip.

1 stalk celery, sliced ¼ inch thick on the diagonal (about ½ cup)

½ cup green olives, pitted and very thinly sliced

2 teaspoons capers, rinsed and drained

1 cup Sweet and Sour Peppers and Onions (page 94)

¼ cup currants or raisins

2 tablespoons crushed smoked almonds

2 tablespoons chopped mixed fresh herbs (parsley, mint, dill)

Kosher salt

Fresh ground black pepper

4 rounds whole wheat pita, cut into eighths, or 4 cups tortilla chips

Bring a pot of water to a boil and add the celery, olives, and capers. Cook until the celery is soft enough to pierce with a fork. Drain. Combine the celery mixture, peppers and onions, currants, almonds, and herbs in a mixing bowl and stir until thoroughly mixed. Season with salt and pepper. Transfer to a serving bowl and serve with the pita or tortilla chips. The dip will keep, tightly covered, in the refrigerator for up to 2 weeks.

NOTE: To make Sicilian caponata from this point just add some pan-fried eggplant. Cube the eggplant in ½-inch cubes and fry on all sides until soft. Don't be afraid if eggplant gets a little more color than you think necessary. It will be beyond the golden brown that most books discuss.

CHICKEN SCALOPPINE WITH PEPPERS AND ONIONS

Serves 4

The peppers and onions become a sauce in this one-pot dinner: Sear the breasts in a saucepan, remove them, then heat the peppers and onions with wine and water in the same pot. Return the breasts to the pot to finish the cooking.

4 (5-ounce) boneless, skinless chicken breasts, pounded thin
Kosher salt
Fresh ground black pepper
½ cup rice flour or Wondra quick-cooking flour
1 tablespoon canola oil, plus more if needed
4 to 8 cloves garlic, thinly sliced
1 cup white wine
2 cups Sweet and Sour Peppers and Onions (page 94)
4 teaspoons Garlic Puree (page 141)
2 cups cooked brown rice
Extra virgin olive oil for drizzling

Season the chicken breasts on one side with salt and pepper and on the other with just the salt. Sprinkle rice flour on one side of each breast.

Heat the canola oil in a large saucepan over medium-high heat. Slide the floured side of one chicken breast into the pan and cook until the edge is opaque and the center is light pink. Using a slotted spatula, transfer the chicken to a plate and repeat with the remaining chicken breasts, adding more canola oil if the pan is dry.

Add the sliced garlic to the pan and cook until soft and fragrant. Add 1⅓ cups water, the wine, peppers and onions, and garlic puree and season with salt and pepper. Stir until thoroughly mixed. Return the chicken breasts to the pan, pink side down. Cook, spooning the sauce over the breasts, until they are cooked through and the sauce thickens.

Spoon ½ cup brown rice on each plate, arrange a chicken breast over each, and spoon some sauce over. Drizzle with olive oil and serve.

Serves 4

This dish is in heavy rotation in my house because the preparation (chopping the garlic and herbs) takes less than 5 minutes. The rest involves cooking the ingredients in a skillet in stages—and you're done.

8 boneless, skinless chicken thighs, patted dry and pounded ¼ inch thick
Kosher salt
Fresh ground black pepper
2 tablespoons canola oil
4 cloves garlic, thinly sliced
½ cup white wine
2 cups Sweet and Sour Peppers and Onions (page 94)
1 cup oil-cured olives, pitted
4 teaspoons Garlic Puree (page 141), optional
¼ cup chopped mixed fresh herbs (parsley, dill, mint)

Season the thighs with salt and pepper on one side and salt on the other. Heat the oil in a large skillet over medium heat. Slip the thighs in and cook until the edges are opaque and the meat moves easily when you shake the pan. Resist the temptation to move them before they are properly seared. Turn over and cook until browned.

To make the sweet and sour salsa, add the sliced garlic to the pan and sauté until golden and fragrant. Add the wine and cook until it is reduced by half. Add the peppers and onions and 1 cup water and distribute evenly in the pan. Stir in the olives and garlic puree, if using. Season with salt and pepper. Simmer until the sauce thickens to the consistency of ketchup and the chicken is falling off the bone, about 20 minutes. Stir in the herbs. Transfer the chicken and sauce to a platter and serve warm.

POUND IT OUT

Chicken thighs (and breasts for that matter) are thinner around the edges than they are in the middle, which means they cook unevenly unless you pound them into a uniform thickness. To do this, place the chicken between two pieces of plastic wrap or waxed paper that are several inches larger than the thigh or breast and use a meat pounder (or a rolling pin) to pound the meat to the desired thickness.

Serves 4

I call this a stir-fry because the cooking is fast and furious. If the shrimp are entirely opaque before the sauce is heated through, remove them with a slotted spoon to prevent them from overcooking, then return them to the pan when the sauce is warmed through.

20 large (15/20 per pound) shrimp, tail on, peeled and deveined
Kosher salt
Fresh ground black pepper
¼ cup Spicy Red Rub (page 55)
Canola oil for the pan
4 cloves garlic, thinly sliced
1 tablespoon extra virgin olive oil, optional
¼ cup red wine vinegar or ½ cup water
4 cups Sweet and Sour Peppers and Onions (page 94)
¼ cup Garlic Puree (page 141)
4 cups broccoli florets, blanched and shocked (see page 62)
¼ cup chopped scallions, white and light green parts only

Season the shrimp with salt and pepper. Sprinkle with the red rub to coat all over. Heat a large skillet slicked with canola oil over medium heat. Add the shrimp and cook until seared (they will turn dark pink) on one side. Add the sliced garlic to the pan along with 1 tablespoon olive oil if the pan is dry and turn the shrimp to sear on the other side. When the garlic is soft and fragrant, add the vinegar or water. Stir in the peppers and onions and garlic puree and cook until heated through.

Meanwhile, warm the broccoli in the microwave, or steam in a pot fitted with a steamer and enough water to cover the bottom until it is just warmed through. Arrange the broccoli on a plate and spoon the shrimp and peppers over it. Scatter the scallions over and serve hot.

NOTE: You can easily substitute chicken tenders for shrimp here. My kids love this combination.

Serves 4

Sushi-grade tuna is ideal here because you want to be able to eat it cooked to medium rare, with just a sear on the outside. Avoid cooking it at a super-high heat; medium high is just right. The peppers and onions are a condiment here; bring them to room temperature before serving with brown rice.

4 (6-ounce) sushi-grade tuna steaks, about ½ inch thick
Kosher salt
Fresh ground black pepper
¼ cup Spicy Red Rub (page 55)
¼ cup canola oil
¼ cup red wine vinegar
2 cups Sweet and Sour Peppers and Onions (page 94)
1 cup Tomato Sauce (page 174)
¼ cup chopped mixed fresh herbs (parsley, mint, dill)

Season the tuna with salt and pepper on one side and just salt on the other side. Spread the rub on a piece of parchment paper and press all sides of the tuna into it and shake off excess.

Heat the oil in a large skillet over medium-high heat. Slip the steaks into the pan and sear on both sides, about 90 seconds per side for medium rare. Transfer the tuna to a warm plate.

Add the vinegar to the pan and, using a wooden spoon, scrape up the bits that have stuck to the pan. Add ½ cup water, the peppers and onions, and tomato sauce and cook until the liquid is reduced by half. Stir in the herbs. Arrange a tuna steak on each of four dinner plates, spoon some of the sauce over, and serve.

NOTE: I love this dish over steamed or grilled broccoli with a squeeze of fresh lemon or the now infamous Ladolemono sauce.

MEDITERRANEAN SALSA

Makes 2 cups / Serves 4

There's just no comparison between this homemade version of salsa and the jarred stuff.

**2 cups Sweet and Sour Peppers
 and Onions (page 94), chopped**
2 tablespoons chopped fresh cilantro
2 tablespoons crumbled feta cheese
Whole wheat pitas, cut into triangles,
 or tortilla chips, for dipping

In a medium bowl, combine the peppers and onions, cilantro, and feta and stir to incorporate. Transfer to a serving bowl and serve with pita or tortilla chips. The salsa can be stored, tightly covered, in the refrigerator for up to 2 weeks.

TUNA SUSHI WITH MEDITERRANEAN SALSA

Makes 20 pieces / Serves 4

This dish combines Italian crudo with sushi rice to create what I call Mediterranean sushi. No soy sauce!

1¼ cups Brown Sushi Rice (page 41)
4 ounces sushi-grade tuna, sliced
 ¼ inch thick against the grain on an
 angle
Extra virgin olive oil for rubbing
**Scant ½ cup Mediterranean Salsa
 (above)**
Scant 2 tablespoons crumbled
 feta cheese
Kosher salt
Fresh ground black pepper
2 tablespoons chopped mixed fresh
 herbs (parsley, mint, dill)
Red wine vinegar for drizzling

Wet your hands and scoop 1 tablespoon of the rice into one palm. Make a fist around it to shape into a ½- x 1-inch rectangle. Push the ends in with your thumb and index finger to create clean edges. Put the rice block on a platter and repeat with remaining rice.

Drape a slice of tuna over each rice block, then rub with olive oil. Top with a teaspoon of salsa and ¼ teaspoon feta, and season with salt and pepper. Garnish with a pinch of the herbs and a drop of the vinegar. Serve immediately.

SPICY EGG WHITE SCRAMBLE

Serves 4

Gently folding over the egg whites onto themselves—to sandwich the heat in the middle of the layers and delicately cook them—is the key to a tender scramble. Gentle is the key word here; if you push the eggs around too vigorously, they will look curdled (although they'll taste fine). Nail down the technique and you'll have the base for endless versions of a scramble.

Extra virgin olive oil for the skillet
2 cloves garlic, sliced
1 cup Sweet and Sour Peppers and Onions (page 94)
½ teaspoon kosher salt
¼ teaspoon fresh ground black pepper
4 large egg whites (½ cup), whisked until foamy
4 basil leaves, chopped
2 small pepperoncini with seeds, chopped
Chipotle Yogurt Sauce (page 51) for drizzling, optional
Crumbled feta cheese for garnish, optional

Slick a 10-inch nonstick pan with just enough olive oil to thinly coat the bottom. Add garlic and sauté over medium heat until golden brown. Add the peppers and onions and cook until the liquid from the mixture evaporates. Season with the salt and pepper.

Distribute the mixture evenly over the bottom of the pan. Add the egg whites and sprinkle the basil and pepperoncini over. With a rubber spatula, gently fold the egg whites from the edge of the pan to the middle of the mixture every 30 seconds, working around the pan. Cook and fold until the eggs are just set.

Divide the scramble among four plates and spoon some chipotle sauce and feta on top, if desired. Serve warm.

SWEET AND SOUR PEPPERS AND ONIONS

SPICY CHICKEN TACOS

Serves 4

The flavor of the peppers and onions is so intense that they only need the addition of heat (through the spice mix and the rub) to create a flavor-packed filling for tacos. Garlic puree and white vinegar amp up the sweet and sour flavors even more.

1 pound ground chicken

2 tablespoons canola oil

6 cloves garlic, thinly sliced

1 tablespoon Gyro Spice Mix (page 53)

1 tablespoon Spicy Red Rub (page 55)

2 cups Sweet and Sour Peppers and Onions (page 94)

2 tablespoons white vinegar

Kosher salt

Fresh ground black pepper

1 tablespoon Garlic Puree (page 141)

8 (6-inch) corn or seven-grain tortillas, warmed

¼ cup Chipotle Yogurt Sauce (page 51)

Combine the chicken, oil, sliced garlic, spice mix, and red rub in a medium pot over medium-high heat. Cook, breaking up the chicken with a spoon and distributing the spices evenly throughout. Stir in 2 cups water, the peppers and onions, and vinegar and season with salt and pepper. Bring the mixture to a boil, reduce the heat, and stir in the garlic puree. Simmer until the mixture has thickened and the liquid has evaporated almost entirely. Divide among the tortillas and serve warm with the chipotle sauce.

NOTE: This recipe also makes killer quesadillas. Just sprinkle a little cheese over the top, cover with another tortilla, and toast in the oven.

BULGUR SALAD WITH OLIVES AND DATES

Makes about 5 cups / Serves 4

This spin on classic tabbouleh is not only a textural dream, but it takes your palate on that fantastic roller coaster ride from sweet to sour to salty to herbaceous to briny. The salad is fantastic on its own for lunch and can easily become dinner by adding a little leftover grilled chicken, steak, or salmon (see variation below).

⅔ cup dry bulgur
Boiling water
2 cups My Favorite Vegetable Dip (page 96)
¼ cup pitted and halved oil-cured black olives
4 Medjool dates, pitted and cut lengthwise into slivers
⅔ cup diced unpeeled cucumber
¼ cup diced red onion
2 tablespoons finely chopped mixed fresh herbs (parsley, mint, dill)
6 tablespoons red wine vinegar
2 tablespoons extra virgin olive oil
Kosher salt
Fresh ground black pepper

Put the bulgur in a bowl and pour enough boiling water over just to cover. Cover and let sit until all of the liquid is absorbed, 25 to 30 minutes.

Combine the cooked bulgur with the dip, olives, dates, cucumber, onion, and herbs in a serving bowl and toss. Add the vinegar and olive oil and toss again. Season with salt and pepper and serve.

VARIATION: WITH PULLED SALMON

Grill 4 (4- to 5-ounce) salmon fillets, then pull them apart into bite-sized pieces. Add the salmon pieces along with an additional 2 teaspoons extra virgin olive oil and ¼ cup red wine vinegar to the salad and toss. Season again to taste with salt and pepper.

Serves 4

Pounding a chicken breast very thin is a genius technique if you are in a hurry because it makes it cook so fast. Here, it is coated with an addictive spicy rub. Watch the chicken carefully as it grills; it can burn easily, so preheat just to medium to get a good sear.

Canola oil for the grill
4 (5-ounce) skinless, boneless
   chicken breasts, pounded thin
Kosher salt
Fresh ground black pepper
¼ cup **Gyro Spice Mix (page 53)**
¼ cup **Red Wine Vinaigrette (page 192)**
2 to 3 cups **Bulgur Salad with
   Olives and Dates (page 108)**
1 lemon, halved
Extra virgin olive oil for drizzling,
   optional
¼ cup **Cucumber Yogurt Dip
   (page 37) or store-bought tzatziki,
   optional**

Preheat a gas grill or grill pan over medium heat. Rub the grates or pan with canola oil. Season the chicken breasts with salt and pepper and sprinkle both sides with the spice mix. Grill on one side until the edges are opaque, about 2 minutes, then flip and grill on the other side, 2 minutes more. Transfer to a plate.

To serve, arrange a breast on a dinner plate, drizzle a little vinaigrette over and top with salad. Squeeze fresh lemon juice over, drizzle with a little olive oil if desired, and serve with yogurt dip if desired.

VARIATION: WITH SPICY PRAWNS

Preheat oven to 500°F. Season prawns with salt, pepper, and spice mix. Place on baking sheet slicked with canola oil and roast for 5 minutes. Plate as above.

ROASTED CHERRY TOMATOES

ROASTED CHERRY TOMATOES

WHEN I WAS AT ANTHOS, THE RESTAURANT FOR WHICH I RECEIVED A MICHELIN star, I used to roast cherry tomatoes just for their delicious juice. I pureed them, tied them up in cheesecloth, and used all the liquid that dripped through to make a tomato gelée that I draped over raw fish. This was taking roasted tomatoes to the extreme and isn't suited for everyday home cooking. But the point is, those tiny roasted globes are a source of such intense flavor that they can transform any dish.

At home, you can get all of the flavor and none of the fuss by leaving the tomatoes whole. Slide them into the oven while you are roasting something else. Making them requires so little effort—toss in olive oil, season with salt and herbs, roast—that their huge payoff seems criminal.

I love the roasted tomato recipe here because it features the quintessential Mediterranean flavors of garlic, extra virgin olive oil, and oregano. But there's that juice, too, released by the roasted tomatoes, that should be poured into the storage container along with the bits that have stuck to the pan. If I have to make a case—other than convenience and incomparable flavor—for preparing these in advance, it's that they get better with time. They will keep in the refrigerator for up to a week and in the freezer, tightly sealed, for up to 2 months.

If you have roasted tomatoes in the refrigerator, you have an antipasto ready for serving, and can make the most satisfying snack simply by putting them on a piece of good bread with some feta sprinkled on top. Almost any protein, salad, or grain dish will benefit from a fistful of roasted tomatoes tossed in. Or use them in a fresh salad to reshape the whole idea of tossed greens—add shaved pecorino and some Red Wine Vinaigrette (page 192) and prepare ho-hum salads no more. And for a quick side dish, leave the tomatoes whole and toss them with fingerling potatoes to serve with any protein.

Pureed, roasted tomatoes make a delectable soup (page 116). Add almonds, vinegar, and herbs to make a pesto (page 125) that can be drizzled over meat or tossed into pasta. (Pesto is incomparably flexible: It can be eaten hot or cold; spooned onto chicken, fish, or beef; spread onto a sandwich; and tossed into pasta. It also grows in flavor as it sits.)

I offer a healthier version of the dinner my mother made on the nights she was in a pinch, when there was soccer practice, ballet, and chorus to get to. She would make a scramble of tomatoes, feta, French fries, and herbs. Even in a rush, she would hand cut the fries and fry them in olive oil and drain them on paper towels. But once she had her batch of fries, the whole thing took less than 15 minutes. Skip the fries; the frittata based on my mother's quick fix (page 123) is so good on its own you don't need them.

As in every other chapter, I have adopted culinary concepts from all over the world and used Mediterranean flavors to create my Live to Eat dishes. Such is the case with the scallop sushi (page 126): A dollop of cherry tomato pesto on each disk adds an outrageous amount of flavor. In. A. Tiny. Drop.

Say the word *tomato* and of course pasta comes to mind, so I've also included a pasta recipe here (page 127) that reinforces the idea of flopping the ratio of vegetable to pasta, so that you get more of the good and good-for-you stuff (tomatoes) and less of the pasta, yet never feel unsatisfied.

The reason I use cherry tomatoes—and cherry tomatoes alone—is that they have the perfect balance of tart and sweet, and they are of good quality year-round. Of course, those offered at summer farmstands or at the greenmarket are ideal. Look for organic versions whenever possible and always make more than you think you will use.

ROASTED CHERRY TOMATOES

Makes about 4 cups

Buy fresh organic cherry tomatoes if possible and feel free to use the golden or orange varieties; they taste slightly different (sweeter, less acidic) and add color and excitement. Stay away from the pear or grape versions. These are meant to show off their unusual shapes and are best enjoyed raw.

3 tablespoons extra virgin olive oil
3 cloves garlic, minced
½ teaspoon dried oregano
1 teaspoon kosher salt
Pinch fresh ground pepper
3 pints cherry tomatoes

Preheat the oven to 350°F.

Combine all ingredients in a large bowl and toss to coat the tomatoes. Spread out on a roasting pan and roast until the tomatoes start to shrivel and blister, 10 to 12 minutes.

Transfer the tomatoes, their juices, and any bits that are stuck to the pan to a rigid container with a tight-fitting lid. Refrigerate for up to 1 week. To freeze, label and date quart-size resealable freezer bags. Turn the top inside out and spoon the tomatoes into the bag. Squeeze the bag to release any air and seal. The tomatoes will keep, frozen, for up to 2 months.

WITH ROASTED CHERRY TOMATOES IN YOUR REFRIGERATOR, YOU CAN MAKE:

Spicy Roasted Salmon with Chipotle Yogurt Sauce (page 57)
Roasted Tomato Soup (page 116)
Salmon Sushi with Warm Roasted Tomatoes and Basil (page 117)
Grilled Fillet of Branzino with Warm Roasted Tomatoes, Cauliflower, and Olives (page 119)
Whole Wheat Spaghetti with Roasted Tomato Sauce (page 121)
Egg White Frittata with Roasted Tomatoes, Feta, and Fresh Herbs (page 123)
Roasted Tomato Pesto (page 125)
Skewered Chicken and Shrimp over Greens (page 202)

ROASTED TOMATO SOUP

Serves 4 as a main course, 6 as an appetizer

I don't know if this is more flavorful than elegant, or the other way around. Whatever the case, kids will go for it even though it is more sophisticated than a standard tomato soup.

3 tablespoons canola oil
5 cloves garlic, thinly sliced
28 Roasted Cherry Tomatoes (page 114) with their juices
3 cups Tomato Sauce (page 174)
Kosher salt
Fresh ground black pepper
3 tablespoons Garlic Puree (page 141)
2 tablespoons red wine vinegar
10 oil-cured olives, pitted and chopped
1 tablespoon crumbled feta cheese
1 tablespoon chopped mixed fresh herbs (parsley, mint, dill)
Extra virgin olive oil for drizzling

Combine the canola oil and sliced garlic in a large pot over medium heat and sauté until the garlic is golden brown. Add $1\frac{1}{3}$ cups water, the roasted tomatoes, and tomato sauce and season with salt and pepper. Cook until the sauce is heated through.

Remove from the heat and stir in the garlic puree and vinegar. Transfer the mixture to a blender (in batches if necessary) and, holding the lid on with a kitchen towel, puree the soup until super smooth. (Or use an immersion blender and puree directly in the pot.)

Ladle the soup into bowls and garnish with the olives, feta, and herbs and drizzle with the olive oil. Serve hot.

VARIATION: Cool soup and use as a virgin bloody Mary over ice to get your day going. You can skip the feta, herbs, and oil if you like.

Makes 20 pieces / Serves 4

Pop the tomatoes in the microwave for 30 seconds to warm them through, then drizzle the juices over the sushi after topping with the tomato. You may substitute fluke, mackerel, bass, or scallops for fantastic results.

1¼ cups Brown Sushi Rice (page 41)

4 ounces sushi-grade salmon, sliced against the grain on an angle into ⅛-inch-thick rectangles (½- x 1-inch)

Extra virgin olive oil for rubbing

10 Roasted Cherry Tomatoes (page 114), halved and warmed

Kosher salt

Fresh ground black pepper

Wet your hands and scoop 1 tablespoon of the rice into one palm. Make a fist around it to shape into a ½- x 1-inch rectangle. Push the ends in with your thumb and index finger to create clean edges. Put the rice block on a platter and repeat with remaining rice.

Drape a slice of salmon over each rectangle, then rub with olive oil. Top with a roasted tomato half and drizzle the juices over. Season with salt and pepper. Garnish with the basil and serve immediately.

VARIATION: Add a sprinkle of feta cheese and a slice of olive and you've just created Greek Salad Sushi.

GRILLED FILLET OF BRANZINO WITH WARM ROASTED TOMATOES, CAULIFLOWER, AND OLIVES

Serves 4

This dish, a quintessential Mediterranean fish simply prepared with quintessential Mediterranean ingredients, is typical of the healthy diet of the region. It has converted many once non-fish-eating patrons of my restaurants. You can substitute any fish for the branzino.

2 tablespoons extra virgin olive oil, plus more for the fillets
4 (1- to 1¼-pound) branzino, filleted and skin side patted dry
Kosher salt
Fresh ground black pepper
1 cup cauliflower florets, blanched and shocked (see page 62)
1 cup Roasted Cherry Tomatoes (page 114) with their juices
24 oil-cured olives, pitted
4 teaspoons chopped mixed fresh herbs (parsley, mint, dill)
¼ cup Ladolemono (page 161)
Juice of 1 lemon

Preheat a gas grill or grill pan over medium heat.

Rub olive oil all over the fillets and season the skin side with salt and pepper and the flesh side with just salt. Grill, skin side down, until the edges just begin to become opaque. Using a metal spatula, rotate each fillet 45 degrees and continue to grill on the skin side. When the fish is opaque down the middle, turn it over and grill for 1 minute on the flesh side.

Meanwhile, heat 2 tablespoons of the olive oil in a skillet over medium heat. Add the cauliflower and cook, turning occasionally, until browned in spots, about 2 minutes. Add the tomatoes, olives, and herbs and season with salt and pepper. Cook just until warmed through.

To serve, spoon the tomato mixture onto a plate and arrange a fillet, flesh side down, over it. Drizzle with ladolemono and lemon juice. Serve warm.

Serves 4

A simple classic is made healthier and more flavorful (and thus more satisfying) by amping up its two primary ingredients: tomatoes and garlic. As good as it is on its own, this is what I call a kitchen sink dish. There's room for broccoli or cauliflower if you have it on hand, or leftover roast chicken. Rifle through your fridge and add whatever you find.

1 pound whole wheat spaghetti
¼ cup canola oil
8 cloves garlic, thinly sliced
40 Roasted Cherry Tomatoes (page 114) with their juices
3 cups Tomato Sauce (page 174)
¼ cup Garlic Puree (page 141)
Kosher salt
Fresh ground black pepper
¼ cup extra virgin olive oil
20 large basil leaves, chopped
3 tablespoons pecorino cheese, optional
¼ cup crumbled feta cheese, optional

Cook the spaghetti according to package directions and drain.

Meanwhile, combine the canola oil and sliced garlic in a large sauté pan over medium heat and sauté until the garlic is soft and golden. Add 2 cups water, the roasted tomatoes, tomato sauce, and garlic puree and cook for 3 minutes. Season with salt and pepper.

Add the drained spaghetti to the pan and continue to cook, tossing the pasta occasionally, until the tomato sauce clings to the pasta. Drizzle the olive oil over, add the basil, and toss to incorporate. Transfer the pasta to a large serving bowl and sprinkle with the pecorino and feta, if using. Serve warm.

VARIATION: PASTA PRIMAVERA

Add any vegetables you may have in the fridge or freezer and you just made an Italian-American classic.

EGG WHITE FRITTATA WITH ROASTED TOMATOES, FETA, AND FRESH HERBS

Serves 4

Intensely flavored add-ins—roasted tomatoes, pungent cheese, and bright herbs—are all it takes to turn fluffy egg whites into a meal. Stuff a wedge of this into a warm pita and wrap in foil if you need breakfast—or lunch or dinner—on the go.

1 tablespoon canola oil

4 cloves garlic, thinly sliced

2 cups Roasted Cherry Tomatoes (page 114) with their juices

¼ cup chopped mixed fresh herbs (parsley, mint, dill)

Kosher salt

Fresh ground black pepper

16 egg whites (2 cups), beaten until foamy

3 tablespoons crumbled feta cheese

Preheat the oven to 500°F.

Combine the oil and garlic in a 10-inch non-stick ovenproof skillet over medium heat and sauté until the garlic begins to brown. Stir in the tomatoes and herbs and season with salt and pepper. Distribute the tomatoes evenly in the pan. Pour the egg whites over and sprinkle with the feta. Transfer to the oven and bake until the egg whites are set, 6 to 10 minutes; they shouldn't jiggle when you shake the pan. Let cool until the eggs are fully set. Cut the frittata into wedges and serve warm.

ROASTED TOMATO PESTO

Makes 3 cups

A pesto is made by combining almost any greens or cooked vegetable with herbs, nuts, cheese, and olive oil and whirring it all up in the blender. Eating this version is like getting a mouthful of the Mediterranean in every bite.

2 cups Roasted Cherry Tomatoes (page 114) with their juices
1 cup crushed smoked almonds
1 cup extra virgin olive oil
¼ cup white vinegar
2 cloves garlic, sliced
1 tablespoon chopped mixed fresh herbs (parsley, mint, dill)
2 teaspoons kosher salt
½ teaspoon fresh ground black pepper

Combine the tomatoes and their juices, the almonds, olive oil, vinegar, garlic, herbs, salt, and pepper in a blender or in the bowl of a food processor and pulse until the mixture is just slightly chunky. The pesto will keep, tightly covered and refrigerated, for up to 2 weeks, or in the freezer for up to 2 months.

WITH ROASTED TOMATO PESTO IN YOUR REFRIGERATOR, YOU CAN MAKE:
Scallop Sushi with Roasted Tomato Pesto (page 126)
Pasta with Chicken and Roasted Tomato Pesto (page 127)
Roasted Shrimp with Roasted Tomato Pesto (page 129)
Grilled Chicken Scaloppine with Peppers, Zucchini, and Roasted Tomato Pesto (page 131)
Garlic Grilled Sirloin with Roasted Tomato Pesto (page 133)

SCALLOP SUSHI WITH ROASTED TOMATO PESTO

Makes 20 pieces / Serves 4

Tell the fishmonger you want *dry* scallops, which means they haven't been injected with preservatives that make them wet. Those scallops tend to shrink by half and bleed a milky substance when you cook them. Even worse, they don't brown properly. A dry scallop smells like the ocean and is slightly tacky to the touch.

1¼ cups Brown Sushi Rice (page 41)
4 dry sushi-grade sea or diver scallops (see headnote), patted dry, each thinly sliced crosswise into 5 rounds
Extra virgin olive oil for rubbing
Scant ½ cup Roasted Tomato Pesto (page 125)
Kosher salt
Fresh ground black pepper
Chopped mixed fresh herbs (parsley, mint, dill) for garnish

Wet your hands and scoop 1 tablespoon of the rice into one palm. Make a fist around it to shape into a ½- x 1-inch rectangle. Push the ends in with your thumb and index finger to create clean edges. Put the rice block on a platter and repeat with the remaining rice.

Drape a slice of scallop over each rectangle, then rub with olive oil. Spoon a teaspoon of the pesto onto each and season with salt and pepper. Garnish with the herbs and serve immediately.

Serves 4

Both whole roasted and pureed tomatoes make up the intensely flavored tomato salsa in this dish. Don't take the pan off the heat until the pesto clings to the pasta. If you're not patient, your sauce will slip off of it with every bite.

2 cups shaped pasta, such as fusilli, orecchiette, or penne
¼ cup extra virgin olive, oil plus more for drizzling
4 cloves garlic, thinly sliced
¾ cup Roasted Cherry Tomatoes (page 114) with their juices
3 cups Roasted Tomato Pesto (page 125)
¼ cup Garlic Puree (page 141)
Kosher salt
Fresh ground black pepper
8 chicken tenders, cut crosswise into ½-inch pieces
¼ cup chopped fresh basil
¼ cup crumbled feta cheese

Cook the pasta according to package instructions. Drain.

Meanwhile, heat the oil in a large skillet over medium heat. Add the sliced garlic and sauté until soft and fragrant. Add the tomatoes and sauté for about a minute, using a spoon to break them up. Add 2 cups of the pesto, the garlic puree, and ¼ cup water and season with salt and pepper. Add the chicken and cook until it is opaque and the sauce is reduced by half.

Add the drained pasta to the pan and cook, shaking the pan occasionally, until the sauce clings to the pasta and all of the liquid is absorbed. Add the remaining 1 cup pesto to the pan along with the basil and a drizzle of olive oil and toss to incorporate. Transfer the pasta to a large serving bowl and scatter the feta over. Serve warm.

ROASTED CHERRY TOMATOES

Serves 4

This dish is perfect for experimenting with flavors: If you want a purely Mediterranean dish, skip the spices and let the pesto do all of the work; to add a bit of heat, use the red rub; or make a Middle Eastern–inspired dish by using the gyro spices. Serve with Simple Steamed Broccoli (page 79), Broccoli with Crispy Garlic (page 80), or Grilled Broccoli (page 83), and some brown rice.

20 large (15/20 per pound) shrimp, peeled and deveined
½ cup extra virgin olive oil
Kosher salt
Fresh ground black pepper
½ to ¾ cup Spicy Red Rub (page 55) or Gyro Spice Mix (page 53), optional
1 cup Roasted Tomato Pesto (page 125)

Preheat the oven to 500°F.

Toss the shrimp in ¼ cup of the olive oil, then season with salt and pepper on one side and just salt on the other. Sprinkle the rub or spice mix all over the shrimp, if using. Transfer to a roasting pan in a single layer and roast until the shrimp is opaque, about 5 minutes. To serve, spoon some pesto on a dinner plate and arrange the shrimp over. Drizzle the remaining ¼ cup olive oil over and serve.

GRILLED CHICKEN SCALOPPINE WITH PEPPERS, ZUCCHINI, AND ROASTED TOMATO PESTO

Serves 4

This is a summertime favorite at my house, but it is also ideal if you need a little sunshine on the dinner plate in the dead of winter. The presentation—layering the chicken, vegetables, and pesto in a short stack—is a little chef-y, but it's easy and makes for a really good-looking dish.

4 (5-ounce) boneless, skinless chicken breasts, pounded thin and halved crosswise
Kosher salt
Fresh ground black pepper
1 medium zucchini, sliced on the diagonal into ¼-inch-thick slices
Extra virgin olive oil for brushing
4 roasted red pepper halves
¾ cup Roasted Tomato Pesto (page 125)
4 teaspoons chopped mixed fresh herbs (parsley, dill, mint)

Preheat the oven to 400°F. Preheat a gas grill or grill pan over medium-high heat.

Season the chicken with salt and pepper on one side and just salt on the other. Brush one side of each zucchini slice with olive oil and season with salt and pepper.

Grill the zucchini, oiled side down, until char marks appear. Turn the slices over and grill on the other side until char marks appear. Set aside.

Grill the chicken, in batches if necessary, until the edges are opaque, about 1 minute. Turn over and grill until no longer pink, about 1 minute more. Transfer the chicken to a platter and cover to keep warm.

To assemble each serving, place one chicken breast piece on a dinner plate and top with a pepper half, followed by 1 tablespoon pesto, a second piece of chicken, and 4 slices zucchini. Top with 2 more tablespoons pesto and finish with a drizzle of olive oil and a sprinkling of the herb mix. Serve warm.

ROASTED CHERRY TOMATOES

Serves 4

I suggest using hanger or flat iron steak here because they are among the most flavorful, are considerably less expensive than cuts like strips and rib eyes, and have a "chew" to them that I love. Slice hanger and flat iron steaks against the grain; otherwise, they are tough to chew. Serve with brown rice.

1½ pounds hanger or flat iron steaks or 4 (6-ounce) strip steaks
Kosher salt
Fresh ground black pepper
¼ cup extra virgin olive oil
4 cloves garlic, thinly sliced
24 cloves Garlic Confit (page 138)
1 lemon, halved
½ cup Roasted Tomato Pesto (page 125)
1 teaspoon chopped mixed fresh herbs (parsley, mint, dill)

Preheat a gas grill or grill pan over medium heat.

Season the steaks with salt and pepper on one side and just salt on the other. Grill to desired doneness. Let rest for about 8 minutes.

Meanwhile, heat the olive oil in a skillet over medium heat. Add the sliced garlic and sauté until golden brown. Add the garlic confit and cook, stirring, until heated through.

Cut the meat into ½-inch slices, slicing at an angle against the grain. Spread the garlic mixture over the steak slices and squeeze the lemon juice over. Drizzle the pesto over and garnish with the herbs.

WHEN IS THE STEAK DONE?

Figuring out when a steak is cooked the way you like is as easy as using an electric thermometer. Buy one and you are golden. Here's my rule of thumb: If you have a 1-inch-thick steak and you want it cooked to medium rare, the internal temperature should read 135°F off the fire and the steak should rest for 8 minutes (during which time it will continue to cook and the temperature will rise to 140°F).

Resting is essential. It allows the juices that fled from the surface of the meat when it met the heat to redistribute throughout the meat. You know a steak has rested if it doesn't bleed when you cut into it. For the most flavorful steak, let it rest and then pop in a 400°F oven for less than a minute to warm.

GARLIC CONFIT

GARLIC CONFIT

LITTLE MORE THAN PEELED GARLIC CLOVES SLOW COOKED IN A MIX OF olive and canola oil, garlic confit has become my near-universal replacement for butter. Confiting mellows raw garlic, removing its bite and making it sweet, soft, and unctuous.

Chefs use tons of butter because it makes everything taste better. But it's not altogether necessary. Try adding garlic confit when you make pan sauces (it adds body and flavor, just like butter!), use it as a spread for sandwiches (it's spreadable and savory, just like butter!), and enrich a broth with it (it dissolves when heated, just like butter!).

For me, using garlic confit in place of butter has been life changing. It will transform the way you cook in as many ways as you use butter, while improving your health. Garlic confit is the kind of pantry item every home cook needs: huge flavor payoff with barely any effort. Garlic confit and puree are in every one of my restaurants; I've used them in my Michelin-starred restaurant as well as my less formal places.

When I began trying to come up with ways to make silken sauces without resorting to unhealthy fats, I started by pureeing confited vegetables, which worked beautifully. But when I tried the same technique with garlic, I was floored. There was no going back. It seems that whenever I make a dish in a pan, I find myself reaching for the cloves or puree, adding them by the tablespoonful to the liquid in the pan to give it another layer of flavor. In fact, garlic confit is a perfect example of how I like to build layers of flavor into a dish; you can sauté raw garlic in the confit oil, then add the puree to the pan to intensify the overall effect.

With garlic confit on hand, you can go from using the cloves whole in a garlicky roast chicken (page 149), or spread on a chicken sandwich (page 143), or puree and stir into practically any pan dish to make an unctuous pan sauce, or spread on slices of whole grain bread for the best garlic bread (page 157) you've ever had in your life (no exaggeration).

Or make linguine in the richest clam sauce (page 153); or more accurately, it's (more) clams in (less) linguine, and in just 10 minutes. This pasta reinforces the practice of flopping the ingredient proportions in keeping with the Mediterranean approach to pasta as a side dish.

When I began thinking about the confit as a replacement for butter, the Greek in me turned directly to phyllo, which is generally made flaky with the addition of lots of butter. But rather than try to work with the pastry at all, I took the ingredients in the classic Greek spinach pie known as spanakopita and rolled them up in a tender (and healthier) sole fillet (page 151). It is this kind of thinking that I hope becomes second nature to you as you make your way through *Live to Eat*.

Basically, any time you reach for a fat, resist the urge and pull out your container of garlic confit, use a slotted spoon to remove the cloves, and toss them into your dish. And all of that oil? It carries a tremendous amount of garlic flavor. Use it to make a garlic vinaigrette or Red Wine Vinaigrette (page 192), or slick the pan with it whenever olive oil is called for. You should even cook your scrambled eggs in it.

GARLIC CONFIT

Makes about 3 cups cloves / 5 cups with oil

Confited garlic is nothing more than the peeled cloves slow cooked in a bath of seasoned oil. This strips the raw cloves of their acidity, removes their sharp heat, and concentrates their sweetness. Use these soft cloves anytime butter or garlic is called for in a savory recipe, and especially if raw garlic is too harsh for you.

  Garlic confit will last forever (okay, a month) as long as you put it in a clean jar, refrigerate it, and refrain from double dipping. If the spoonful of confit touches other food, don't put that same spoon back into the jar for more. This calls for 2 cups total of oil. If it isn't enough to cover the garlic cloves completely, add more. To freeze, first puree the cloves (see Garlic Puree, page 141) and store in 3-tablespoon portions in small resealable plastic bags. Let thaw before using.

3 cups peeled garlic cloves
1 fresh bay leaf or 2 dried
8 to 10 sprigs fresh thyme
1 tablespoon kosher salt
1½ teaspoons black peppercorns
1 cup canola oil
1 cup extra virgin olive oil

Preheat the oven to 300°F.

Place garlic cloves, bay leaf, thyme, salt, and peppercorns in a heavy-bottomed, oven-proof pot. Pour the canola and olive oils over to cover. Cover, transfer to the oven, and bake until the garlic cloves are pale gold and tender (you should be able to smash them with the back of a spoon), about 50 minutes. Cool to room temperature.

Transfer the cloves and oil to a clean, wide-mouthed resealable jar.

WITH GARLIC CONFIT IN YOUR REFRIGERATOR, YOU CAN MAKE:
Cucumber Yogurt Dip (Tzatziki; page 36)
Garlic Grilled Sirloin with Roasted Tomato Pesto (page 133)
Garlic Puree (page 141)
Turkey and Mushroom Panini (page 142)
Garlicky Pan-Roasted Chicken (page 149)
Pan-Roasted Chicken with Sun-Dried Tomatoes and Olives (page 181)
Poached Fillet of Sole with Tomato Sauce and Feta (page 185)

GARLIC PUREE

Makes 1 cup

This is simply the smooth, spreadable version of garlic confit. Use it with abandon. Use twice as much as you think you should. Use it instead of mayonnaise on your favorite sandwich. Eat it straight off a spoon (but don't double dip!), standing in front of the fridge.

1 cup Garlic Confit (page 138)

Using a slotted spoon, transfer the garlic cloves only to the bowl of a food processor (a mini-processor is ideal) and process until smooth. Alternatively, mash the cloves with the side of a knife. Store as for Garlic Confit (see page 138).

WITH GARLIC PUREE IN YOUR REFRIGERATOR, YOU CAN MAKE:

Greek Turkey Burgers (page 45)

Garlicky Cauliflower with English Peas and Mint (page 64)

Penne with Cauliflower, Peas, and Pepperoncini (page 66)

Israeli Couscous with Shrimp, Cauliflower, Peas, and Mint (page 70)

Rigatoni with Chicken and Tomato-Stewed Cauliflower (page 73)

Pasta with Sausage and Peppers (page 95)

Chicken Scaloppine with Peppers and Onions (page 97)

Sautéed Chicken Thighs with Sweet and Sour Salsa (page 99)

Spicy Mediterranean Shrimp Stir-Fry (page 101)

Spicy Chicken Tacos (page 107)

Roasted Tomato Soup (page 116)

Whole Wheat Spaghetti with Roasted Tomato Sauce (page 121)

Grilled Chicken Sandwiches with Spinach and Garlic Ricotta (page 143)

Baked Clams à la Grecque (page 144)

Garlic Sauce (page 145)

Littleneck Clams in Garlic Broth (page 147)

Garlicky Pan-Roasted Chicken (page 149)

Baked Fillet of Sole "Spanakopita" (page 151)

Spicy Shrimp with Cauliflower and Broccoli in Garlic Sauce (page 152)

Linguine with Manila Clams (page 153)

Spicy Pork Sofrito with Fennel, Oranges, and Olives (page 155)

Crazy-Good Whole Grain Garlic Bread (page 157)

Chicken with Broccoli, Peas, and Artichokes (page 158)

Rigatoni with Chicken Sausage and Broccoli Rabe (page 159)

Ladolemono (page 161)

Spicy Baked Clams (page 169)

Chicken Scaloppine with Tomato-Artichoke Fondue (page 177)

Whole Wheat Penne with Spinach, Sun-Dried Tomatoes, and Pine Nuts (page 179)

Steamed Clams with Garlicky Tomato Sauce (page 182)

Poached Fillet of Sole with Tomato Sauce and Feta (page 185)

Greek Paella (page 187)

Red Wine Vinaigrette (page 192)

TURKEY AND MUSHROOM PANINI

Serves 4

This sandwich is all about the ingredients. Buy the best fresh turkey available. Deli "cold cuts" are full of preservatives and artificial ingredients. Also, if possible, go for wild mushrooms. The resulting flavor will be worth the price. I love a pressed sandwich, but if you don't have a panini press, you can melt the cheese-topped sandwich halves under the broiler before topping with the ciabatta tops.

½ cup canola oil

3 cloves garlic, sliced

2 cups sliced fresh mushrooms, woody stems removed

Kosher salt

Fresh ground black pepper

9 small sage leaves, chopped

8 large Brussels sprouts, halved, cored, and leaves pulled apart

1 pound thinly sliced turkey

4 ounces Swiss cheese, thinly sliced

6 to 8 cloves Garlic Confit (page 138)

4 ciabatta, halved and toasted

Heat a panini press. Line a tray with paper towels.

Heat the oil in a large skillet over medium heat. Add the sliced garlic and sauté until soft and fragrant. Add the mushrooms and season with salt and pepper. Pan-fry the mushrooms until golden, adding the sage leaves as they brown. Add the Brussels sprout leaves and season with salt and pepper. Sauté until the leaves are slightly caramelized around the edges. Transfer the mixture to the paper towel–lined tray to drain off the excess oil.

Assemble the sandwiches by dividing the ingredients among the four ciabatta bottoms: Begin with the turkey, followed by the mushroom mixture, then the cheese. Spread garlic confit on the four remaining ciabatta pieces, and place on top of the cheese. Press the sandwiches in the hot press, then halve on the diagonal. Serve warm.

GRILLED CHICKEN SANDWICHES WITH SPINACH AND GARLIC RICOTTA

Makes 4

Instead of grilled chicken breasts, you can make the sandwiches with leftover chicken (or turkey if you happen to have that in the fridge). But don't skip toasting the ciabatta; it's essential for it to stand up to the spinach and ricotta.

1 cup ricotta cheese
2 teaspoons Garlic Puree (page 141)
4 teaspoons chopped mixed fresh herbs (parsley, mint, dill)
Kosher salt
Fresh ground black pepper
2 (10-ounce) boneless, skinless chicken breasts, pounded ¼ inch thick
Canola oil for the pan
4 cloves garlic, thinly sliced
4 cups packed baby spinach
4 ciabatta or hearty sandwich rolls, halved and toasted

Preheat a gas grill or grill pan over medium heat. Meanwhile, stir together the ricotta, garlic puree, and herbs to thoroughly incorporate. Season with salt and pepper and set the garlic ricotta aside.

Season each chicken breast with salt and pepper. Grill the breasts for 2 minutes on each side, or until they just lose their pink color, then transfer to a cutting board to rest for at least 2 minutes.

Slick a large skillet with oil, add the sliced garlic, and cook over medium heat until soft and fragrant. Add the spinach, season with salt and pepper, and sauté until the spinach wilts. Blot to remove excess liquid.

Cut the chicken crosswise into ¼-inch-thick slices, holding the knife at an angle. Spread garlic ricotta all the way out to the edge on the bottom half of each ciabatta. Top the ricotta with the spinach and then the sliced chicken. Top with the remaining ciabatta halves and cut the sandwiches in half.

VARIATION: VEGETARIAN SANDWICHES WITH SPINACH AND GARLIC RICOTTA

Instead of the chicken, use your favorite sautéed mushrooms, or tender broccoli florets, either grilled (page 83) or blanched and shocked (page 62).

BAKED CLAMS À LA GRECQUE

Serves 4

This dish is a playful a marriage of the classic Greek spinach pie that everyone loves, spanakopita, and the Italian fan-favorite baked clams oreganata.

2 dozen littleneck clams, scrubbed, any cracked or open clams discarded
1 tablespoon canola oil
2 cloves of garlic, thinly sliced
4 small scallions, white and green parts, finely chopped
2 cups packed spinach, chopped
¼ cup chopped fresh dill
¼ cup crumbled feta cheese
2 tablespoons pecorino romano cheese, optional
Kosher salt
Fresh ground black pepper
Extra virgin olive oil for drizzling
½ cup panko breadcrumbs
Garlic Sauce (facing page)
Lemon wedges, optional

Preheat oven to 350°F. Place the clams on a baking sheet lined with aluminum foil and bake until they open. Remove the clams with spoon, roughly chop them, and return them to half of the shell. Return clams to baking sheet.

Heat the oil in a medium skillet. Add the garlic and scallion and sauté until soft. Add spinach and dill and sauté just until the spinach wilts. Transfer to small bowl. Cool and mix in feta and, if using, pecorino. Season with salt and pepper. Spoon mixture over clams and drizzle with olive oil and a sprinkle of panko. Place in the oven until browned, approximately 5 minutes.

Plate the clams and pour Garlic Sauce over them. Serve immediately, with lemon wedges, if you like.

GARLIC SAUCE

Makes 2½ cups

This is so good you may wind up sipping it by the spoonful. It can be stored, tightly covered, in the refrigerator for up to 10 days.

Canola oil for the pan
4 cloves garlic, thinly sliced
**6 tablespoons Garlic Puree
(page 141)**
2 cups white wine
Juice of 1 lemon
Kosher salt
Fresh ground black pepper

Slick a skillet with canola oil and heat over medium heat. Add the sliced garlic and garlic puree and sauté until the sliced garlic is soft and golden. Add the wine and lemon juice and season with salt and pepper. Cook until the liquid thickens and is the consistency of heavy cream.

Serves 4

I'm not sure which is more satisfying about this dish, eating the tender clams or sopping up the insanely flavorful broth. I like to stir in Israeli couscous, orzo, or fregola (a Sardinian pasta that looks like tiny, rough pebbles) for a hearty dish. Or, you can skip the pasta and serve simply with a whole grain baguette for soaking up the broth. Mussels are a fine substitute; just add a pinch of chile flakes for heat.

Canola oil for the pan

4 cloves garlic, thinly sliced

5½ dozen littleneck clams, scrubbed, any cracked or open clams discarded

1 cup white wine

¼ cup Garlic Puree (page 141), plus more if needed

Kosher salt

Fresh ground black pepper

Juice of 2 lemons

1⅓ cups cooked Israeli couscous, orzo, or fregola

¼ cup chopped scallions

¼ cup chopped mixed fresh herbs (parsley, mint, dill)

Slick a high-sided skillet with canola oil, add the sliced garlic, and sauté over medium heat until soft and fragrant. Add the clams and shuffle them around the skillet for a minute or so. Add the wine, stir in the garlic puree, and season with salt and pepper. Cook until the clams open up; if the liquid reduces by more than half before the clams open, cover the pan until the remaining clams open.

Adjust the flavor of the broth with some lemon juice, additional garlic puree, and salt and pepper to suit your taste. Discard any clams that have not opened. Stir in the couscous, scallions, and herbs and squeeze additional lemon juice over to taste. Serve hot.

Serves 4

Raw, confited, and pureed garlic all come together to make an intensely flavored sauce for seared skin-on chicken breasts—hands down the best crispy chicken *ever*.

4 (10-ounce) bone-in, skin on chicken breasts with wing drumette
Kosher salt
Fresh ground black pepper
Canola oil for the pan
4 cloves garlic, thinly sliced
4 cloves Garlic Confit (page 138)
1 cup white wine
¼ cup Garlic Puree (page 141)
Juice of 1 lemon
¼ cup chopped fresh dill

Preheat the oven to 500°F.

Season the chicken with salt and pepper on the skin side and salt on the other. Slick a high-sided oven-proof skillet with canola oil and heat over medium heat. Arrange the chicken in the skillet, skin side down, and sear. Resist the temptation to move the chicken around. When the breasts move easily when you shake the pan, 3 to 5 minutes, turn over and sear the other side. Turn the breasts over once more so that the skin side is down.

Drain the oil from the skillet and transfer the chicken to the oven. Roast until the juices run clear when you prick the thickest part with a fork, about 8 minutes. Transfer the chicken to a platter.

Drain the fat from the skillet and return to medium heat. Slick with canola oil and add the sliced garlic and garlic confit. Sauté until the garlic is golden and fragrant. Add the wine and stir in the garlic puree. Add the lemon juice and dill and season with salt and pepper. Cook until heated through. Spoon the sauce over the chicken breasts and serve.

NOTE: To get the crispiest skin imaginable, dry the chicken breasts completely with paper towels. If there's time, put the chicken on a baking sheet and refrigerate, uncovered, overnight to completely dry it out. And be sure the oven is preheated before sliding the pan into it.

Serves 4

This is a game changer. Your friends will be amazed.

Canola oil for the pans
4 cloves garlic, thinly sliced
4 cups packed baby spinach
¼ cup chopped scallions
Kosher salt
Fresh ground black pepper
¼ cup crumbled feta cheese
4 (4- to 6-ounce) sole fillets, skin
   removed
1 tablespoon plus 2 teaspoons
   chopped fresh dill
Extra virgin olive oil for drizzling
¾ cup white wine
Juice of ½ lemon
2 tablespoons Garlic Puree (page 141)

Preheat the oven to 500°F. Slick a skillet with canola oil over medium heat. Add one-fourth of the sliced garlic and sauté until golden. Add the spinach and scallions, season with salt and pepper, and cook just until the spinach wilts. Transfer the greens to a paper towel–lined plate to remove excess liquid. Transfer to bowl, add the feta and 2 teaspoons of the dill, and toss. Let the filling cool.

Season the fish fillets with salt and pepper on one side and salt on the other. Arrange them on a rimmed baking sheet, ugly side up. Divide filling among fillets, spooning it lengthwise down the center of each. Roll up like a jelly roll and drizzle with olive oil. Pour ½ cup of the wine into the rimmed baking sheet. Bake until the fish separates slightly when pricked with a fork, about 10 minutes.

Meanwhile, make the sauce: Slick a medium skillet with canola oil and heat over medium heat. Add the remaining sliced garlic and sauté until soft. Add the remaining ¼ cup wine and lemon juice. Stir in the garlic puree. Cook until the liquid is thick enough to coat the back of a spoon.

Add the remaining 1 tablespoon dill and spoon the sauce over the fish.

152

SPICY SHRIMP WITH
CAULIFLOWER AND BROCCOLI IN GARLIC SAUCE

Serves 4

Heat, acidity, brightness, sweetness—there's nothing not to love about this. Feel free to throw some Gyro Spice Mix (page 53) in with the red rub before coating the shrimp if you want to add the warmth of cumin, cardamom, cinnamon, and cloves.

4 cups broccoli and cauliflower
  florets, blanched and shocked
  (see page 62)
20 large shrimp (15/20 per pound),
  tail on, peeled and deveined
Kosher salt
Fresh ground black pepper
¼ cup Spicy Red Rub (page 55)
Canola oil for the pan
1 cup white wine
Juice of 1 lemon
¼ cup Garlic Puree (page 141)

Heat the vegetables in a microwave if they have been chilled in the refrigerator. Season the shrimp with salt and pepper then sprinkle the red rub all over them to coat entirely.

Slick a large skillet with oil and heat over medium heat. Slide the shrimp into the skillet and cook, turning once, until they take on color on both sides. Add the wine and lemon juice and continue to cook until the shrimp are no longer translucent, about 1 minute. Stir in the garlic puree. If the sauce is thicker than heavy cream, stir in a little water to achieve the desired consistency.

Arrange the broccoli and cauliflower on each of four plates. Divide the shrimp among them and spoon the sauce over. Serve warm.

LINGUINE WITH MANILA CLAMS

Serves 4

More clams, less linguine—that's the Live to Eat way. Using so much shellfish adds tons of flavor to the broth and the garlic puree gives it wonderful body. Use fresh clams here—I've yet to find canned clams that remotely compare, plus, the shells add a nice touch.

1 pound linguine
Canola oil for the pan
8 cloves garlic, thinly sliced
8 pepperoncini with seeds, chopped
Pinch red pepper flakes
5½ dozen manila clams, scrubbed, any cracked or open clams discarded
1⅓ cups white wine
¼ cup Garlic Puree (page 141)
Juice of 1 lemon
Kosher salt
Fresh ground black pepper
¼ cup chopped mixed fresh herbs (parsley, mint, dill)

Cook the pasta according to package directions and drain.

Slick a large skillet with oil and add the sliced garlic and pepperoncini. Sauté over medium heat until the garlic is soft and fragrant. Add the red pepper flakes and clams and sauté for 30 seconds. Add the wine, cover, and cook, shaking the pan occasionally as the clams begin to open. Stir the garlic puree and lemon juice into the pan and season with salt and pepper. Simmer, covered, until all of the clams have opened, 2 to 3 minutes. Stir in the herbs. If the broth is too thick for your taste, add enough water to reach your desired consistency. Discard any clams that have not opened.

Push the clams to one side of the pan and add the drained pasta to the broth. Toss with tongs and transfer the pasta to a large serving bowl. Top with the clams and serve hot.

VARIATION: Use clams, mussels, and shrimp for a seafood extravaganza.

Makes 4

Take care not to overcook the pork tenderloin, which is extremely lean and very tender—the center should be slightly pink when you remove it from the pan (it is returned to the pan in the end to quickly finish cooking). If you have one, use a mandoline to slice the fennel into whisper-thin slices, otherwise, use a very sharp knife.

2 oranges or grapefruits, or a mix
2 cups shaved fennel (on a mandoline, or sliced paper thin with a very sharp knife)
12 Greek olives, pitted and halved
Kosher salt
Fresh ground black pepper
All-purpose flour for dredging
1½ pounds pork tenderloin, cut into ½-inch-thick slices and pounded to a ¼-inch thickness
2 tablespoons canola oil, plus more as needed
8 cloves garlic, thinly sliced
¼ cup capers, rinsed and drained
8 pepperoncini, with or without seeds, thinly sliced
Pinch red pepper flakes
2 cups white wine
½ cup Garlic Puree (page 141)

Segment the oranges or grapefruits (see page 12) over a large bowl to catch the juices. Add the fennel and olives to the bowl and season with salt and pepper. Set the salad aside.

Sprinkle flour on one side of each tenderloin slice and shake off the excess. Heat the canola oil in a large skillet over medium heat. Working in batches, slip the tenderloins, floured side down, into the pan and sauté until the edges lose their pink color and the centers are light pink. Transfer the slices to a plate and continue sautéing the remaining pork, adding oil to the pan as necessary.

Add the sliced garlic, capers, and pepperoncini to the pan and sauté until the garlic is soft and begins to take on color. Stir in the pepper flakes. Add the wine and stir in the garlic puree. If the sauce is thicker than the consistency of heavy cream, stir in enough water to thin it. Add the pork back to the pan, pink side down, and cook for about 30 seconds, until the pink color disappears.

Divide the pork among four dinner plates and spoon the pan sauce over. Top with the orange-olive-fennel salad and serve.

Makes 4

I'd eat garlic bread for breakfast if my wife would let me, but it is more in keeping with the Mediterranean diet if you serve it with any dish in which tomato sauce or a garlicky broth plays a role (perhaps Steamed Clams with Garlicky Tomato Sauce, page 182). Dense, seeded breads with a chewy crumb work well here.

1 whole grain baguette (about 16 inches long)
Extra virgin olive oil for drizzling
Kosher salt
Fresh ground black pepper
Spicy Red Rub (page 55), optional
Garlic Puree (page 141), for spreading

Heat the broiler with a rack in the middle of the oven. Cut the bread in half crosswise and then horizontally to make 4 pieces (like a submarine sandwich). Drizzle olive oil liberally on the cut side of each piece and season with salt and pepper. If you want a spicy garlic bread, lightly sprinkle red rub on each.

Place the bread on a baking sheet, oiled side up, and toast 5 inches under the broiler until the bread has a light golden crust. Spread each piece of bread with the garlic puree as you would butter, pushing it out to the edges. Return the bread to the oven and broil just until the puree is warmed through. Serve warm.

FOR MORE GARLIC PUNCH, use sautéed garlic in addition to whole garlic confit cloves. Heat 1 tablespoon extra virgin olive oil in a small pan over medium-low heat. Add 2 cloves thinly sliced garlic and 8 to 10 cloves garlic confit. Sauté until the slices are crisp and the confit takes on color. Add a pinch of red chile flakes. After broiling the bread the first time, use a slotted spoon to top two pieces of the bread slices with the garlic mixture and generously season with salt. Top with the remaining bread slices to make two sandwiches. Slice crosswise into 1-inch-thick pieces.

CHICKEN WITH BROCCOLI, PEAS, AND ARTICHOKES

Serves 4

This is reminiscent of the chicken and broccoli dishes you find in Chinese restaurants—but with Mediterranean flavors. It's universally loved, and is best when you use good-quality imported artichokes. Chicken tenders cook quickly; take care not to overcook them. Serve over brown rice.

Canola oil for the pan
4 cloves garlic, thinly sliced
¾ cup Garlic Puree (page 141)
Kosher salt
Fresh ground black pepper
1¼ pounds chicken tenderloins, cut
   into ½-inch pieces
**8 cups broccoli florets, blanched
and shocked (see page 62)**
1⅓ cups artichoke hearts packaged in
   water, drained
1 cup green peas, thawed if frozen
1 lemon, halved

Slick a large skillet with the oil and heat over medium heat. Add the sliced garlic and sauté until soft and fragrant. Add 1⅓ cups water, stir in ½ cup of the garlic puree, and season with salt and pepper. Add the chicken and cook until it loses its pink color, shaking the pan occasionally. As the chicken nears the end of cooking, add the broccoli, artichokes, and peas and cook until heated through. Stir in the remaining ¼ cup garlic puree. Squeeze the lemon juice over, and serve warm.

Serves 4

A classic dish, but with modern proportions. Always use a short pasta for this dish so that you can catch all of the ingredients in one bite. Leave the seeds in the pepperoncini if you want a super spicy sauce.

2 cups whole wheat rigatoni or other shaped pasta

Canola oil for the pot

8 small pepperoncini, with or without seeds, chopped

8 cloves garlic, thinly sliced

4 cups broccoli rabe, blanched and shocked (see page 62), cut into bite-sized pieces

½ cup Garlic Puree (page 141)

¾ pound chicken sausage (about 3 links), cut into ½-inch pieces

Kosher salt

Fresh ground black pepper

Grated pecorino cheese, optional

Crumbled feta cheese, optional

Cook the pasta according to package directions. Drain, reserving 2 cups of the pasta water.

Wipe out the pot with paper towels, slick with canola oil, and heat over medium heat. Add the pepperoncini and sliced garlic and sauté until the garlic is soft and fragrant. Add 2 cups water, the broccoli rabe, and ¼ cup of the garlic puree, then add the sausage. Cook until the sausage loses its pink color. If the liquid in the pan has evaporated, add enough of the reserved pasta water to the pot so that it will coat all of the ingredients.

Transfer the pasta to the pot and stir in the remaining ¼ cup garlic puree. Cook, tossing, until the sauce clings to the pasta. Season with the salt and pepper and serve warm with the cheeses for garnish, if desired.

Makes 4 cups

It may sound chef-y but here goes: Store this super-simple Greek sauce in a squeeze bottle and you will use it *all the time*. I find I want to drizzle the tangy, unctuous lemon-oil sauce on just about everything; it makes a more exciting dressing than just a squeeze of lemon. Toss with some blanched vegetables for an instant side dish, spoon it on top of grilled meats, pork, and chicken, or use it as a marinade for any protein.

1 cup lemon juice

3 tablespoons Garlic Puree (page 141)

1 tablespoon Dijon mustard

¼ teaspoon dried oregano

2 tablespoons kosher salt

½ teaspoon black peppercorns, ground very fine

2⅓ cups extra virgin olive oil

Whisk together the lemon juice, garlic puree, mustard, oregano, salt, and pepper in a large bowl until thoroughly combined. Slowly drizzle in the oil, whisking until thoroughly incorporated. Store, tightly covered, in the refrigerator for up to 2 weeks.

WITH LADOLEMONO IN YOUR REFRIGERATOR, YOU CAN MAKE:

GRILLED SWORDFISH

Serves 4

Use sushi-grade swordfish and cook it to medium rare for the most tender, juicy results. If that's too rare for you, the farthest you want to cook swordfish is to medium; to do this, pull it off the heat when it is slightly underdone and let it rest to fully cook through.

This is great with an Heirloom Tomato Salad (page 199) or a simple broccoli dish (see pages 80 and 81) and brown rice.

4 (6-ounce) sushi-grade swordfish steaks, ½ inch thick
Kosher salt
Fresh ground black pepper
8 teaspoons Spicy Red Rub (page 55), or to taste (optional)
Canola oil for the pan
¼ cup Ladolemono (page 161)
¼ cup chopped fresh mixed herbs (parsley, mint, dill)

Season the swordfish with salt and pepper on both sides. If using rub, dredge to cover both sides. Heat a large skillet slicked with oil over medium heat. Slip the steaks into the pan and cook until opaque halfway up the edges, about 2 minutes. Flip the fish over and cook until the remainder of the edges are opaque, about 2 minutes more. Transfer the steaks to each of four dinner plates. Drizzle the ladolemono over and sprinkle with the herbs. Serve warm.

SCALLOP SUSHI WITH MINT

Makes 20 pieces / Serves 4

Top-quality scallops, fresh mint, lime juice, and ladolemono—it's as simple as that for a huge flavor payoff.

1¼ cups Brown Sushi Rice (page 41)
4 dry sushi-grade diver scallops (see headnote, page 126), patted dry and thinly sliced into 20 rounds
Extra virgin olive oil for rubbing
Juice of 2 limes
Sea salt
Fresh ground black pepper
Ladolemono (page 161) for drizzling
Fresh mint (tiniest leaves possible or chopped) for garnish

Wet your hands and scoop 1 tablespoon of the rice into one palm. Make a fist around it to shape into a ½- x 1-inch rectangle. Push the ends in with your thumb and index finger to create clean edges. Put the rice block on a platter and repeat with the remaining rice.

Drape a slice of scallop over each rectangle, then rub with olive oil. Drizzle with the lime juice and season with salt and pepper. Drizzle with ladolemono and garnish with the mint. Serve immediately.

Serves 4

This combination is the Greek answer to meat and potatoes, with lamb chops instead of steak, and Mediterranean flavors (and healthier choices) standing in for the standard American potato toppings of butter, bacon, and sour cream. Ask your butcher to cut a rack of lamb into chops for you.

4 russet baking potatoes, washed and patted dry
1 (8-rib) rack of lamb, cut into chops
Extra virgin olive oil for the chops
Kosher salt
Fresh ground black pepper
2 lemons, halved
½ cup Ladolemono (page 161)
½ cup Cucumber Yogurt Dip (page 37) or store-bought tzatziki
3 tablespoons chopped mixed fresh herbs (parsley, mint, dill) or chopped chives

Pierce potatoes with fork and cook in microwave per manufacturer's instruction. Set aside.

Meanwhile, preheat a gas grill or grill pan over medium heat. Rub the chops on both sides with olive oil, then season with salt and pepper on one side and salt on the other.

Grill the chops until they are nicely seared, about 1½ minutes per side for medium rare. Transfer the chops to a cutting board to rest. Grill the lemon halves, cut side down, until charred.

Arrange two lamb chops and a baked potato on each of four dinner plates. Drizzle the ladolemono over the chops. Split the potatoes open and spoon some yogurt dip into each, then top with the herbs. Serve warm with the charred lemons.

VARIATION: SALT-BAKED POTATO

A layer of salt in the baking sheet not only holds the potatoes in place but gives the potatoes a lightly salted crust. Preheat the oven to 350°F. Pour a ¼-inch-thick layer of kosher salt in a rimmed baking sheet. Pierce each potato 2 or 3 times and place on the salt. Bake until a fork pierces the potatoes easily, 50 to 60 minutes.

GRILLED SPICY CHICKEN KEBABS WITH WILTED SPINACH

Serves 4

Poultry (and other meats) coated in spice rubs can burn easily at high heat, but the temperature is necessary to get a good sear on the chicken pieces. So, watch them closely and grill just until seared, then let them rest to complete the cooking.

2 (10-ounce) boneless, skinless chicken breasts or thighs, cut into 1-inch pieces

Ladolemono (page 161) for marinating and finishing

½ cup Spicy Red Rub (page 55) or Gyro Spice Mix (page 53)

16 bamboo skewers, soaked in water for at least 15 minutes

2 tablespoons extra virgin olive oil

8 cloves garlic, thinly sliced

4 cups packed spinach

4 teaspoons chopped mixed fresh herbs (parsley, mint, dill), optional

Kosher salt

Fresh ground black pepper

Cucumber Yogurt Dip (page 37) or store-bought tzatziki, optional

Put the chicken in a large resealable plastic bag and add enough ladolemono to cover. Seal the bag and marinate for at least 30 minutes or overnight in the refrigerator. Transfer the chicken to a baking sheet and sprinkle the red rub or spice mix over the pieces, turning to coat all sides. I like to use both, 50/50. Discard the marinade.

Preheat a gas grill or grill pan over high heat. Thread four pieces of chicken onto each skewer and grill, turning as soon as the edges are opaque, until almost cooked through, about 3 minutes. Transfer to a plate to rest.

Meanwhile, heat the olive oil in a large skillet over medium heat. Add garlic and sauté until soft. Add the spinach and the herbs. Season with salt and pepper. Cook, tossing, until the spinach is wilted.

Divide the spinach in the center of four dinner plates and top with two skewers of chicken. Drizzle with ladolemono. Serve with the cucumber dip, if desired.

VARIATION: SPICY CHICKEN PITAS

Skip the spinach and serve the chicken in warm pitas drizzled with **Ladolemono** and a dollop of **Cucumber Yogurt Dip.** Serve with a green salad.

ROASTED SHRIMP WITH
KALE, FENNEL, AND RED ONION SALAD

Serves 4

Baby kale stays firm under the weight of any dressing, yet it's still soft enough to eat and far less bitter than its bigger counterpart. If you can't find baby kale, chop mature kale into bite-sized pieces.

20 large shrimp (15/20 per pound),
   tail on, peeled and deveined
Canola oil for the shrimp
Kosher salt
Fresh ground black pepper
4 cups packed baby kale
1 cup shaved fennel (on a mandoline,
   or sliced paper thin with a very
   sharp knife)
½ cup slivered red onions
2 ounces pecorino cheese, shaved
½ cup Ladolemono (page 161)

Preheat the oven to 500°F.

Rub the shrimp all over with oil and season with salt and pepper. Place on a baking sheet and roast until the shrimp is opaque, about 5 minutes. Remove the tails from the shrimp.

Combine the kale, fennel, onion, and pecorino in a salad bowl. Pour the lado-lemono over and toss to coat. Season with salt and pepper.

Divide the salad among four dinner plates and arrange the shrimp on top. Alternatively, slice the shrimp in half lengthwise and add it to the bowl with the greens. Toss to incorporate into the salad and serve.

VARIATION: ROASTED SPICY SHRIMP

For a spicy alternative, sprinkle **½ cup Spicy Red Rub (page 55)** on the shrimp to coat all over before roasting them.

168

ROASTED SALMON WITH
BRUSSELS SPROUT AND FENNEL SALAD

Serves 4

Think of Brussels sprouts as baby cabbages. Rather than steam or roast them, you can eat them raw. Just peel the leaves apart.

20 large Brussels sprouts, halved, cored, stems removed, and leaves peeled apart

2 cups shaved fennel (on a mandoline, or sliced paper thin with a very sharp knife)

½ cup chopped mixed fresh herbs (parsley, mint, dill)

½ cup Ladolemono (page 161), plus more for drizzling

Kosher salt

Fresh ground black pepper

Canola oil for the pan

4 (5-ounce) skin-on salmon fillets, patted dry

Lemon wedges, for serving

Preheat the oven to 500°F.

Combine the Brussels sprout leaves in a bowl with the fennel and ¼ cup of the mixed herbs. Add the ladolemono and toss to coat. Season with salt and pepper and set aside.

Coat a roasting pan with canola oil. Season both sides of the salmon fillets with salt and pepper. Put them in the pan, turn to coat all over with the oil, and place skin side down. Roast 10 minutes for medium rare (the interior will be jewel toned and the surface of the flesh will be soft orange and opaque).

Arrange some Brussels sprout salad on each of four dinner plates and top with a salmon fillet, skin side up. Drizzle a little ladolemono over and sprinkle with the remaining ¼ cup mixed herbs. Serve warm with lemon wedges.

VARIATION: Grilled or pan-roasted swordfish, tuna, or halibut would be totally different but exciting options here.

SPICY BAKED CLAMS

Serves 4

These are addictive. Period.

2 dozen littleneck clams, scrubbed, any cracked or open clams discarded

1 cup diced Roasted Cherry Tomatoes (page 114) with their juices

4 pepperoncini, with or without seeds, chopped

½ teaspoon dried oregano

Kosher salt

Fresh ground pepper

Extra virgin olive oil for drizzling

½ cup panko breadcrumbs

Garlic Sauce (page 145)

Pinch of Spicy Red Rub (page 55), optional

Lemon wedges, optional

Preheat the oven to 350°F.

Place the clams on a baking sheet lined with aluminum foil and bake until they open. Remove the clams with spoon, roughly chop them, and return them to half of the shell. Return clams to baking sheet.

In a small mixing bowl, combine tomatoes, pepperoncini, and oregano. Season with salt and pepper and spoon evenly over prepared clams. Finish with a drizzle of olive oil and a sprinkle of panko. Place in the oven until browned, approximately 5 minutes.

Plate the clams and pour Garlic Sauce over them. Sprinkle with Red Rub and garnish with lemon wedges if you like.

TOMATO SAUCE

TOMATO SAUCE

Mᴘᴊ ʟᴏᴠᴇ ᴏғ ᴛᴏᴍᴀᴛᴏ ᴀᴀᴜᴄᴇ ɪᴏ ʙᴏʀɴᴇ ᴏᴜᴛ ᴏғ ᴛʜᴇ Aᴍᴇʀɪᴄᴀɴ ɪɴғʟᴜᴇɴᴄᴇ in my otherwise traditional Greek upbringing, as Italian food was so popular—especially where I grew up in New York. Whenever I wasn't eating Greek food, I was drawn to classic Italian stews, braises, ground meats, and, of course, pasta dishes in which tomato sauce figured prominently. Unlike her Italian counterparts, my mother never made Sunday sauce, but she did turn out big batches at the end of the summer, when the tomatoes overflowed in our garden.

Yes, a previous chapter featured roasted cherry tomatoes, and you can make a quick sauce by pulverizing them (see Roasted Tomato Pesto, page 125). But a sauce made from quality canned plum tomatoes, with a little garlic and basil and vinegar, is versatile in ways that roasted cherry tomatoes are not.

Tomato sauce is one of my favorite ingredients to play with in the restaurant kitchen. Such a simple lineup of ingredients—canned tomatoes, basil, garlic, red wine vinegar—belie tomato sauce's remarkable taste. While there's nothing like sitting down to a piping hot bowl of pasta with tomato sauce, I have found plenty of other more healthful ways to exploit its incomparable flavor and texture. In this chapter, you will learn how to create simple pan sauces, fondues, and braises as well as easy pasta dishes in which the ratio of what I like to call the "good stuff"—vegetables, seafood, whatever else is added in—is greater than the pasta. One of my favorite ways to use tomato sauce is to add white wine to it as it heats in the pot to make what I like to call a "fondue" (page 177). Technically, it's not used for dunking into but rather I add all kinds of vegetables to the bubbling sauce to coat them with what eventually becomes a delectable dip.

Making tomato sauce requires little active cooking time—most of it is spent simmering in the pot. Make a lot at a time because it freezes beautifully. But, if you find yourself drawn to a recipe that calls for tomato sauce and you come up short, it's okay to use a top-quality jarred variety in a pinch.

Note that the tomato sauce is thinned with wine and water to become a pan sauce—a technique that is very useful when you want a light sauce to spoon over almost any protein or cooked vegetable.

TOMATO SAUCE

TOMATO SAUCE

Makes about 12 cups

The success of your tomato sauce depends heavily on the quality of the canned tomatoes. I choose San Marzano because they have the most natural acidity.

This sauce is equally delicious thick and chunky as it is silky and smooth. If you want to have both styles on hand, reserve some before pureeing the rest. It will keep, tightly covered, for up to 1 week in the refrigerator and up to 3 months in the freezer.

⅓ cup extra virgin olive oil

20 small cloves garlic, crushed

4 (28-ounce) cans imported good-quality peeled plum tomatoes in their juice

15 basil leaves

1 tablespoon plus 2 teaspoons kosher salt

¼ teaspoon fresh ground black pepper

Red wine vinegar to taste

In a large pot, heat the oil and garlic over medium-high heat until the garlic is softened. Add the tomatoes and 6 cups water, give a stir, and bring to a boil. Reduce the heat and simmer, uncovered, until the sauce clings to a wooden spoon, about 1½ hours.

Stir in the basil and crush the tomatoes with the back of the spoon. Season with the salt and pepper. Taste and add enough vinegar to achieved your desired acidity. I like a tangier sauce, so I'm a bit heavy-handed with the vinegar. To make the sauce smooth at this point, puree in a blender.

Tip: If you are going to puree the sauce, doing so before you begin the cooking process will result in a much brighter red color.

WHOLE WHEAT SPAGHETTI WITH GARLICKY TOMATO SAUCE

Serves 4

Comfort food, in reasonable portions.

1 pound whole wheat spaghetti
1 tablespoon extra virgin olive oil,
   plus more for drizzling
10 cloves Garlic Confit (page 138)
2 cloves garlic, thinly sliced
¼ cup white wine
1½ cups Tomato Sauce (page 174),
   left chunky
8 basil leaves, chopped

Cook the spaghetti according to package instructions. Drain.

Combine the oil, garlic confit, and sliced garlic in a large saucepan over medium heat and sauté until the garlic slices are soft and fragrant. Add the wine and cook until the liquid is reduced by half.

Add the tomato sauce and cook until it is reduced by half. Toss the drained pasta in the sauce and let it sit briefly on the heat, stirring occasionally, until the liquid is thoroughly absorbed and the sauce clings to the pasta. Drizzle with olive oil and toss in the basil leaves. Serve warm.

NOTE: Adding sweet herbs at the end of the cooking process allows them to bloom in the heat of the sauce. Releasing their fragrances is like breathing spring into the dish.

CHICKEN SCALOPPINE WITH TOMATO-ARTICHOKE FONDUE

Serves 4

The trick here is to add just enough liquid to the tomato sauce to create a smooth, light, delicate "fondue"—thick enough to coat the vegetables but not so thick that it overwhelms them, much like a traditional cheese fondue. Keep an eye on the pan as the liquid is reducing and return the chicken to the pan when the sauce is just thick enough to cling to the artichokes.

4 (5-ounce) boneless, skinless
   chicken breasts, pounded to a
   ¼-inch thickness and halved
Kosher salt
Fresh ground black pepper
All-purpose flour for dredging
Canola oil for the pan
1⅓ cups artichoke hearts packaged in
   oil, drained
4 cloves garlic, thinly sliced
1 cup frozen peas
¾ cup Tomato Sauce (page 174),
   pureed
¼ cup Garlic Puree (page 141)
¼ cup chopped fresh dill
Extra virgin olive oil for drizzling

Season the chicken with salt and pepper on one side and just salt on the other. Dredge one side of each piece of chicken with flour and shake off excess. Slick a large skillet with canola oil and heat over medium-high heat. Working in batches, slide the chicken, floured side down, into the pan and sauté until the edges are opaque and the center remains pink. Using a slotted spoon, transfer the chicken to a plate. Slick the pan with more canola oil if necessary between batches.

Add the artichokes and sliced garlic to the pan and sauté until the garlic is soft and fragrant. Stir in 1 cup water, the peas, tomato sauce, garlic puree, and dill and season with salt and pepper. Reduce the sauce until it clings to a spoon. Return the chicken to the pan and cook until the chicken is cooked through, about 1 minute. Arrange the chicken on a platter and spoon the sauce over. Drizzle the olive oil over and season to taste with salt and pepper.

WHOLE WHEAT PENNE WITH
SPINACH, SUN-DRIED TOMATOES, AND PINE NUTS

Serves 4

When you need a quick pasta dish that comes together right in the pot, look no further.

3 cups whole wheat penne or other
   short pasta
Canola oil for the pan
2 cloves garlic, thinly sliced
**2 cups Tomato Sauce (page 174),
   left chunky**
1 pound pre-cooked chicken sausage,
   cut into ½-inch pieces
6 sun-dried tomatoes, drained and
   chopped
4 cups packed baby spinach,
   chopped
¼ cup Garlic Puree (page 141)
¼ cup pine nuts, toasted
Kosher salt
Fresh ground black pepper
¼ cup chopped mixed fresh herbs
   (parsley, mint, dill)
Extra virgin olive oil for drizzling
Grated pecorino cheese, optional

Cook the pasta according to package instructions. Drain, reserving 2 cups of the pasta water.

Wipe out the pot, slick with canola oil, and heat over medium-high heat. Add the sliced garlic and sauté until soft and fragrant. Stir in the tomato sauce and 1⅓ cups of the pasta water and cook until the sauce bubbles. It should be smooth and just thick enough to coat a spoon; if it is too thick, gradually stir in more water.

Stir in the sausage. Add the sun-dried tomatoes, spinach, garlic puree, and pine nuts and stir to incorporate. Season with salt and pepper. Stir in the mixed herbs. Add the pasta to the skillet and leave on the heat until the sauce clings to the pasta. Drizzle with the olive oil, toss, and transfer to a serving bowl. Garnish with pecorino if you like and serve.

TOMATO SAUCE

NOTE: If using raw sausage, begin by cooking the sausage in the pan with oil, taking care to add garlic only after the sausage has browned nicely so the garlic does not burn. Remember, it's not necessary to fully cook the sausage as it will continue to cook in the sauce. But do cook it long enough to give it a good sear.

PAN-ROASTED CHICKEN WITH
SUN-DRIED TOMATOES AND OLIVES

Serves 4

This chicken, with the holy trinity of the Greek table—tomatoes, garlic, olive oil—screams *Mediterranean*. I use chicken here, but steak and pork are just as delicious.

4 bone in, skin on chicken breast
  halves (about 2½ pounds)
Kosher salt
Fresh ground black pepper
Canola oil for the pan
8 cloves Garlic Confit (page 138)
2 cloves garlic, thinly sliced
1 cup Tomato Sauce (page 174),
  pureed
½ cup white wine
14 cured black olives,
  pitted and halved
6 sun-dried tomatoes, preferably imported, drained of oil and
  chopped
Extra virgin olive oil for drizzling
8 basil leaves, chopped

Preheat the oven to 450°F.

Season the chicken breasts all over with salt and pepper. Heat a large oven-proof skillet slicked with canola oil over medium-high heat. Lay the breasts in the pan skin side down and sear just until the skin is lightly browned. Turn the breasts over and sear lightly on the other side. Turn the breasts back so that they are skin side down, slide the pan into the oven, and roast the chicken until just cooked through, about 12 minutes. Turn the breasts over and set them aside on a plate to rest.

Return the pan to medium-high heat and stir in the garlic confit, sliced garlic, tomato sauce, wine, and ⅔ cup water. Add the olives and sun-dried tomatoes and season with salt and pepper. Cook until the liquid is reduced by half.

To serve, arrange a chicken breast on each plate and spoon the sauce over. Drizzle with olive oil and garnish with basil.

SAUTEÉD PORK TENDERLOIN WITH SPICY TOMATO-BRAISED BROCCOLI RABE

Serves 4

Pork tenderloin is the filet mignon of pork. Be sure to slice the tenderloin into uniformly thick pieces so that they cook evenly. Don't be afraid of medium pork.

2 (1-pound) pork tenderloins, sliced crosswise into 1-inch-thick slices
Kosher salt
Fresh ground black pepper
Canola oil for the pan
4 cloves garlic, thinly sliced
2 pepperoncini with seeds, chopped
4 cups blanched and shocked broccoli rabe (see page 62), chopped
1 cup Tomato Sauce (page 174), pureed
Extra virgin olive oil for drizzling

Season the tenderloin slices all over with salt and pepper. Slick a large skillet with canola oil and heat over medium heat. Lay the pork in the pan and sear, about 2 minutes on each side. Add the garlic and pepperoncini and sauté until the garlic is soft and fragrant. Add the broccoli rabe, tomato sauce, and 1 cup water and toss to incorporate. Season with salt and pepper. Cook until the liquid is reduced by half.

To serve, spoon the broccoli rabe onto a platter and arrange the pork on top. Finish with sauce and a drizzle of olive oil and serve.

STEAMED CLAMS WITH GARLICKY TOMATO SAUCE

Serves 4

I don't know how you eat this without bread—and perhaps you shouldn't. We all need to splurge every now and then!

2 tablespoons canola oil
4 cloves garlic, thinly sliced
4 cups Tomato Sauce (page 174), left chunky
1 cup white wine

Heat the oil and sliced garlic in a large skillet over medium heat until the garlic is soft and fragrant. Add the wine and reduce by half. Add the tomato sauce, 1⅓ cups water, garlic puree, and salt and pepper

continued

¼ cup Garlic Puree (page 141)

Kosher salt

Fresh ground black pepper

5½ dozen manila clams, scrubbed,
   any cracked or open clams discarded

20 basil leaves, chopped

Extra virgin olive oil for drizzling

and reduce by one-quarter. Add clams and cook until they open. Discard any clams that have not opened. Stir in the basil, drizzle with olive oil, and serve hot.

FUSILLI WITH SHRIMP IN
CHUNKY TOMATO SAUCE WITH SMOKED MOZZARELLA

Serves 4

Combining fish and cheese is not something you find in all Mediterranean countries but it's a very common pairing in Greece. In this pasta, the smoked mozzarella perfumes the entire dish with a delicate smoky flavor.

2 cups fusilli or other short, shaped
   pasta

2 tablespoons canola oil

4 cloves garlic, thinly sliced

1 cup white wine

**4 cups Tomato Sauce (page 174),
   left chunky**

Kosher salt

Fresh ground black pepper

20 large shrimp (15/20 per pound),
   tail on, peeled and deveined

1⅓ cups diced smoked mozzarella

20 basil leaves, chopped

Extra virgin olive oil for drizzling

Grated pecorino cheese for sprinkling

Cook the pasta according to package instructions. Drain, reserving 2 cups of the pasta water.

Wipe out the pot and heat the canola oil and garlic over medium heat. Sauté until the garlic is soft and fragrant. Add wine and reduce by one-quarter. Add the tomato sauce, salt, pepper, and 2 cups pasta water and bring to a simmer. Add the shrimp and cook in the sauce, turning until opaque. Add the mozzarella and pasta, toss to coat, and cook until the sauce clings to the pasta. Toss in the basil. Drizzle with the olive oil and transfer to a serving bowl. Sprinkle the pecorino over and serve warm.

Serves 4

I think of this as Fish 101—easy to prepare and not at all fishy. If you can't find sole, flounder is a perfectly fine substitute.

4 (6-ounce) sole fillets, tails trimmed
   if too long for the pan
Kosher salt
Fresh ground black pepper
All-purpose flour for dredging
Canola oil for the pan
4 cloves garlic, thinly sliced
1 cup white wine
1 cup Tomato Sauce (page 174),
   pureed
24 cloves Garlic Confit (page 138)
1 tablespoon plus 1 teaspoon Garlic
   Puree (page 141), optional
¼ cup chopped fresh dill
Juice of 1 lemon
¼ cup crumbled feta cheese

Season the fillets with salt and pepper. Press the flesh side of the fillets into the flour and shake off the excess. Slick a large skillet with oil and heat over medium heat. Slip the fillets in the pan, floured side down, and sauté until the edges are opaque. Add the sliced garlic and sauté until soft and fragrant. Stir in 1 cup water, the wine, tomato sauce, garlic confit, and garlic puree. Reduce the heat and bring the liquid to a simmer. Stir in the dill. Simmer until the fish is opaque, then transfer to a platter. Stir the lemon juice into the sauce and spoon the sauce over the fillets. Garnish with the feta and serve.

NOTE: This dish works great with shrimp but could also work with chicken, pork, or veal scaloppine.

GREEK PAELLA

Serves 4

Paella traditionally takes a long time to prepare, but this version goes fairly rapidly when you have tomato sauce and garlic puree on hand.

I call it Greek because it features the flavors of the cuisine, as well as orzo, a quick-cooking Greek pasta, rather than the traditional rice as the base. If you want to skip the merguez, add a tablespoon of either Spicy Red Rub (page 55) or chipotle peppers in adobo sauce to the pan just as the sliced garlic begins to brown.

3 tablespoons canola oil

½ cup chopped merguez sausage

4 cloves garlic, thinly sliced

28 mussels, scrubbed and debearded, any cracked or open mussels discarded

20 littleneck clams, scrubbed, any cracked or open clams discarded

1 cup Tomato Sauce (page 174), pureed

Kosher salt

Fresh ground black pepper

2 cups cooked orzo

8 large shrimp (15/20 per pound), peeled and deveined

2 tablespoons Garlic Puree (page 141)

¼ cup chopped mixed fresh herbs (parsley, mint, dill)

Extra virgin olive oil for drizzling

Heat the canola oil and sausage in a large skillet over medium-high heat until the sausage is lightly browned and its spices visibly infuse themselves into the oil. Add the sliced garlic and sauté until golden. Add the mussels and clams and toss to distribute throughout the pan. Add the tomato sauce and ½ cup water and season with salt and pepper. Add the orzo and stir to incorporate.

When the clams and mussels begin to open, add the shrimp and rotate them in the pan so that they are at the bottom, close to the heat. Add the garlic puree and herbs and stir to incorporate. Check the shrimp for doneness—they should be opaque just through to the center. Discard any shellfish that have not opened. Drizzle some olive oil over and toss with a spoon. Transfer the paella to a rimmed platter and serve warm.

RED WINE VINAIGRETTE

RED WINE VINAIGRETTE

VINAIGRETTES ARE ESSENTIAL TO THE MEDITERRANEAN WAY OF COOKING and eating, and thus to my plan for you. This one is so simple to make, yet it lends a distinct layer of flavor to every dish it is in. Garlic puree and Dijon mustard give it wonderful body, not to mention intense flavor. Plus, it's healthy.

The ratio of oil to acid in a traditional vinaigrette is generally 3 parts oil to 1 part vinegar. But I find this mixture lacking in zing, and invariably add more vinegar; usually a ratio that is somewhere between 3-to-1 and 2-to-1. This is particularly key in the following recipes, in which the vinaigrette is used in myriad ways.

Salads are the obvious beneficiaries of tangy vinaigrette; in the Mediterranean, cooks love to put a protein and salad on the same plate so that the juices from the meat mingle with the vinaigrette, creating an exciting plate sauce that you can mop up with a tangle of greens or swish the meat through. But as with other essentials, my goal is to inspire you to expand its uses in your everyday cooking. Think of it as a condiment that can give almost any dish an unmistakable spark. Its bright acidity breathes life into a roasted piece of steak, fish, or chicken. You can also add a wonderful layer of flavor to a dish with a final drizzle. In this chapter and throughout the book, I use the vinaigrette frequently to finish a dish. Admittedly, this is something you might expect a restaurant chef to do. But there's a reason we give our food that last flourish: It makes that roller-coaster ride of flavor—the one that I am always trying to achieve in each bite of food I make—even more exciting.

WITH RED WINE VINAIGRETTE IN YOUR REFRIGERATOR, YOU CAN MAKE:

Pickled Beet Salad (page 35)

Haricots Verts with Tomatoes and Feta (page 77)

Arugula with Watermelon, Red Onion, and Feta (page 86)

Spicy Chicken Paillard with Bulgur Salad (page 109)

Modern Greek Salad (page 195)

Traditional Greek Salad (page 196)

Classic Tomato Salad (page 198)

Heirloom Tomato Salad (page 199)

Greek Tabbouleh (page 200)

Skewered Chicken and Shrimp over Greens (page 202)

Tuna Salad Wrap (page 203)

Shaved Fennel, Red Onion, and Grapefruit Salad (page 205)

Niçoise Salad, Greek Style (page 207)

RED WINE VINAIGRETTE

Makes 3 cups

Tasted on its own, this will be aggressively acidic. Keep in mind that it mellows considerably when it is used to dress vegetables or is tossed with greens. If you want to tame it even more, drizzle a little extra virgin olive oil on the dressed salad just before serving.

You may find that the vinaigrette mellows over time; to give it a boost, squeeze a little fresh lemon juice into it. It will keep for weeks, tightly covered, in the refrigerator

¾ cup red wine vinegar
1 tablespoon finely diced shallot
2½ teaspoons Dijon mustard
2½ teaspoons Garlic Puree (page 141)
½ teaspoon minced garlic
½ teaspoon dried oregano
1 tablespoon kosher salt
½ teaspoon fresh ground black pepper
1½ cups canola oil
¼ cup extra virgin olive oil

Combine the vinegar, shallot, mustard, garlic puree, minced garlic, oregano, salt, and pepper in a blender and puree on medium speed until smooth. With the motor running, slowly add the canola and olive oils in a thin stream and blend until thoroughly incorporated. Transfer to a large container with a tight-fitting lid and refrigerate.

NOTE: If you are making extra portions of a big salad, do not toss it with the vinaigrette before storing in the refrigerator. Keeping the salad separate from the vinaigrette will extend its life.

MODERN GREEK SALAD

Serves 4

Greeks never put greens in their Greek salads (see Traditional Greek Salad, page 196). But I understand the impulse—who wouldn't want to add the crunch of romaine to the mix?

4 cups packed ¼-inch strips of hearts
   of romaine
3 medium red bell peppers, diced
2 medium cucumbers, diced
2 medium tomatoes, cored and diced
1 large red onion, diced
1⅓ cups crumbled feta cheese
1⅓ cups Greek olives, pitted and halved
¼ cup chopped mixed fresh herbs
   (parsley, mint, dill)
½ cup Red Wine Vinaigrette (page 192)
Kosher salt
Fresh ground black pepper
Extra virgin olive oil for drizzling

Combine the romaine, bell peppers, cucumbers, tomatoes, onion, feta, olives, and herbs in a large bowl and toss. Add the vinaigrette and toss to coat the vegetables. Season with salt and pepper, then drizzle olive oil over the top.

VARIATION: WITH GRILLED HANGER STEAK

Pat dry a 1½-pound hanger steak, season with salt and pepper, and grill over high heat to desired doneness, turning once, about 12 minutes total for medium rare. Let the steak rest for at least 8 minutes.

For dinner, slice the steak on the diagonal into ¼-inch slices. Divide the salad among four plates, arrange the steak slices on top, and drizzle with additional vinaigrette.

RED WINE VINAIGRETTE

TRADITIONAL GREEK SALAD

Serves 4

Greeks eat this salad family style, served on a large platter at the same time the main course and other side dishes are served. A typical menu would combine the salad with grilled lamb chops and some rice.

2 medium heirloom tomatoes, cored
  and cut into 1-inch pieces
1 small red onion, cut into ¼-inch-
  thick slivers
1 yellow bell pepper, sliced into
  ¼-inch-thick rings, pith removed
1 English cucumber, peeled and cut
  into ¼-inch-thick pieces
4 ounces feta cheese, cut into
  ½-inch cubes
14 oil-cured olives, pitted
2 tablespoons chopped mixed fresh
  herbs (parsley, mint, dill)
½ teaspoon dried oregano
½ **cup Red Wine Vinaigrette (page 192)**
2 teaspoons extra virgin olive oil
Kosher salt
Fresh ground black pepper
12 dolmas (see page 198), optional

Combine the tomatoes, onion, bell pepper, cucumber, feta, olives, fresh herbs, and dried oregano in a large bowl and toss. Add the vinaigrette and olive oil and toss with your hands or a spoon to coat. Season with salt and pepper and serve with the dolmas, if desired.

VARIATION: ROASTED CHICKEN SALAD WRAP

Pull 10 ounces of roasted chicken, skin on, into bite-sized pieces. Make the Traditional Greek Salad, cutting all of the ingredients into small dice. Toss the chicken with the salad along with an additional ¼ **cup Red Wine Vinaigrette** and season with salt and pepper. Divide among 4 (10-inch) whole wheat tortillas, arranging the salad down the middle. Wrap the bottom over the salad, fold in one side, and roll up to the top.

CLASSIC TOMATO SALAD

Serves 4

Make this in the middle of summer when garden tomatoes are bursting with sugary sweetness and tons of juice, which creates a wonderful plate sauce that mixes with the feta and vinaigrette. You will want to lap it up!

2 medium tomatoes, cored and cut into 1-inch pieces
1 small red onion, cut into slivers
8 ounces feta cheese, cut into ½-inch cubes
1 teaspoon dried oregano
1 cup Red Wine Vinaigrette (page 192)
Kosher salt
Fresh ground black pepper
1 tablespoon extra virgin olive oil

Combine the tomatoes, onion, feta, and oregano in a large bowl and toss. Add the vinaigrette and toss with your hands or a spoon to coat. Season with salt and pepper. Drizzle with the olive oil and serve.

DOLMAS: A READY-MADE LIVE TO EAT SNACK

Dolmas, or grape leaves stuffed with rice and herbs, make wonderful, self-contained snacks in addition to accompaniments to salads. The closest to homemade that you can buy are the imported variety packed in olive oil, available at artisanal markets and of course Middle Eastern markets and Greek grocery stores. If they come in a tin, transfer to a plastic container with a tight-fitting lid and they will keep for weeks in the refrigerator.

HEIRLOOM TOMATO SALAD

Serves 4

There is no better salad when tomatoes are in season. Use different varieties of tomato for a visual wow.

6 medium heirloom tomatoes, halved, cored, and cut into bite-sized chunks

1 English cucumber, halved and cut on an angle into ¼-inch-thick slices

1 small red onion, sliced thinly on the mandoline or cut into slivers

¼ cup chopped fresh mixed herbs (parsley, mint, dill)

½ teaspoon dried oregano

1⅓ cups crumbled feta cheese

½ cup Red Wine Vinaigrette (page 192)

1 tablespoon extra virgin olive oil

Kosher salt

Fresh ground black pepper

Combine the tomatoes, cucumber, onion, herbs, oregano, and half of the feta in a large bowl and toss. Add the vinaigrette and olive oil and toss with your hands or a spoon to coat. Season with salt and pepper. Transfer to a serving bowl or platter and scatter the remaining feta over.

VARIATION: WITH GRILLED CHICKEN PAILLARD

Pound four 5-ounce boneless, skinless chicken breasts until thin, season with salt and pepper, and grill until the edges are opaque. Turn and grill for another minute. Place a breast on a dinner plate, drizzle **1 tablespoon Red Wine Vinaigrette** over, and top with some salad.

RED WINE VINAIGRETTE

GREEK TABBOULEH

Serves 4

More vegetables, less bulgur. I eat this at least twice every week, not only because it's healthy, but because it's a textural dream. Add leftover salmon, chicken, or steak for a killer lunch. If you do add a protein, be sure to dress the tabbouleh with a bit more vinaigrette. The tabbouleh will keep, tightly covered, in the refrigerator for 3 days.

1⅓ cups dry bulgur
Boiling water
2 heirloom tomatoes, cored and diced
2 medium cucumbers, diced
1 large red onion, diced
1⅓ cups chopped roasted red peppers
1⅓ cups chopped pitted Greek olives
½ teaspoon dried oregano
½ cup chopped mixed fresh herbs
   (parsley, mint, dill)
⅔ cup crumbled feta cheese
¾ cup Red Wine Vinaigrette (page 192)
Kosher salt
Fresh ground black pepper

Put the bulgur in a bowl and pour enough boiling water over it just to cover. Cover and let sit until all of the liquid is absorbed, about 20 minutes.

Combine the bulgur, tomatoes, cucumbers, onion, roasted peppers, olives, oregano, herbs, and feta in a large bowl and toss. Add the vinaigrette, salt, and pepper, and toss to thoroughly coat. Serve at room temperature.

VARIATION: WITH SEARED GYRO-SPICED TUNA

If you have prepared the tabbouleh, dinner is a quick-seared tuna steak away. I love to put a little extra vinaigrette onto the plate or drizzle it over the tuna so that there's a little bit more happening. Press both sides of 4 (6-ounce) sushi-grade tuna steaks into about **½ cup Gyro Spice Mix (page 53)** and shake off excess. Sear the steaks in a skillet slicked with canola oil over medium heat, about 2 minutes per side. Serve alongside the salad. Drizzle additional vinaigrette over and serve warm.

SKEWERED CHICKEN AND SHRIMP OVER GREENS

Serves 4

Here, the vinaigrette is used both as a marinade for chicken and as a dressing for a simple salad of arugula and fennel.

6 ounces boneless, skinless chicken
  breast, lightly pounded and cut
  into 1½-inch pieces
¾ cup Red Wine Vinaigrette (page 192)
12 large (15/20 per pound) shrimp,
  peeled and deveined, tails removed
Canola oil for drizzling
Kosher salt
Fresh ground black pepper
2 cups packed arugula
½ small fennel bulb, sliced thinly
  on the mandoline or cut into slivers
½ small red onion, sliced thinly
  on the mandoline or cut into slivers
**Roasted Cherry Tomatoes
  (page 114), warmed**
8 (10-inch) wooden skewers

Put the chicken pieces in a resealable plastic bag and pour ½ cup of the vinaigrette over. Seal the bag, shake to coat the chicken pieces, and refrigerate at least 30 minutes or up to 2 hours.

Preheat a gas grill or grill pan over medium heat.

Remove the chicken from the marinade. Drizzle both chicken and shrimp with canola oil, and season with salt and pepper.

Grill the chicken pieces until cooked through, turning once. At the same time, grill the shrimp, turning once, until cooked through, about 1 minute per side. Reserve.

Meanwhile, combine the arugula, fennel, and onion in a bowl, drizzle with the remaining ¼ cup vinaigrette, and toss. Season with salt and pepper.

Thread the chicken and shrimp onto wooden skewers, alternating with roasted tomatoes on each skewer.

Arrange some salad on each plate and place a chicken and shrimp skewer over each.

TUNA SALAD WRAP

Makes 4

Quick. Easy. Healthy. Delicious.

2 (10-ounce) cans top-quality
  Italian tuna in oil
⅔ cup diced peppers
⅔ cup diced peeled cucumber
⅔ cup diced red onion
¼ cup chopped mixed fresh herbs
  (parsley, mint, dill)
**6 tablespoons Red Wine Vinaigrette
  (page 192)**
2 teaspoons extra virgin olive oil
Kosher salt
Fresh ground black pepper
4 romaine leaves
4 (10-inch) whole wheat tortillas

Combine the tuna, peppers, cucumber, onion, fresh herbs, vinaigrette, and olive oil in a bowl and toss to coat thoroughly. Season with salt and pepper. Place one romaine leaf in the center of each tortilla. Divide the salad among the tortillas, wrap the bottom over the salad, fold in one side, and roll up to the top.

VARIATION: Use top-quality canned salmon, crab, or chicken for this quick and easy wrap. I will become a go-to lunch for the kids. Mark my words.

SHAVED FENNEL, RED ONION, AND GRAPEFRUIT SALAD

Serves 4

This is a fantastic winter salad, either as a first course or as a side dish to any kind of fish. Make it a main by topping with a few grilled shrimp.

2 cups packed arugula

2 cups packed thinly shaved fennel (on a mandoline, or sliced paper thin with a very sharp knife)

½ cup slivered red onion

2 grapefruits, segmented with their juices

1 cup oil-cured olives, pitted

¼ cup chopped mixed fresh herbs (parsley, mint, dill)

½ cup Red Wine Vinaigrette (page 192)

Kosher salt

Fresh ground black pepper

Combine the arugula, fennel, onion, grapefruit segments and their juices, olives, and herbs in a large bowl. Drizzle the vinaigrette around the sides of the bowl and toss to coat. Season with salt and pepper and serve.

VARIATION: **SWEET AND SOUR DRIED FRUIT SALAD**

Cut 8 dried apricots into ¼-inch-wide pieces. Pit 4 Medjool dates, then halve and cut into ¼-inch-wide pieces (chill the dates and they'll be easier to chop). Add the apricots and dates to the salad, along with 28 pitted oil-cured olives. Taste, taste, taste as you go—if the salad is too sweet for you, squeeze in a bit of lemon juice at the end. Serve with Roasted Spicy Shrimp (page 167) for a perfect Live to Eat dinner.

Serves 4

A French classic goes Greek with cucumber, feta, and oregano. Make extra fingerlings to have on hand for tossing into tomorrow's lunch or dinner salad. Or, serve them as a side dish with just a drizzle of extra virgin olive oil and a squeeze of lemon or Red Wine Vinaigrette.

4 (6-ounce) tuna steaks
Kosher salt
Fresh ground black pepper
8 to 10 ounces haricots verts,
  blanched and shocked
  (see page 62)
20 Niçoise or other
  oil-cured olives with pits
12 fingerling potatoes, boiled
1 medium heirloom tomato,
  cored and cut into 1-inch chunks
½ English cucumber, peel on, cut
  on the diagonal into ¼-inch slices
½ cup slivered red onion
4 ounces feta cheese,
  cut into ½-inch cubes
2 tablespoons chopped mixed fresh
  herbs (parsley, mint, dill)
½ teaspoon dried oregano
1 cup Red Wine Vinaigrette (page 192)
Extra virgin olive oil for drizzling

Preheat a gas grill or grill pan over medium heat. Season the tuna with salt and pepper on one side and salt on the other. Grill the tuna to medium rare, about 3 minutes on each side.

Meanwhile, combine the haricots verts, olives, potatoes, tomato, cucumber, onion, feta, fresh herbs, and dried oregano and toss. Add ½ cup of the vinaigrette and toss to coat. Season with salt and pepper.

Divide the salad among four dinner plates, placing a tuna steak next to each salad. Drizzle with the remaining ½ cup vinaigrette and olive oil and serve warm.

ACKNOWLEDGMENTS

This book was truly an adventure. It took on a life of its own, but it found its way and became something I am infinitely proud of. I would be remiss if I didn't acknowledge that a family—and I use the word "family" because I believe we became one as we fought and argued our way through the creative process that ultimately produced what I had envisioned—of people helped create this book:

Anna Caputo, my wife, listened to me talk endlessly about the ever-changing process that my mind goes through every time I start a project. It never ends as it begins. Thank you.

Michael Szczerban, my editor at Little, Brown. What can I say? You were undoubtedly the bridge that joined the creative process, helping to guide it to a common ground, listening to my endless requests and changes, buffering the head-butting along the way, and somehow doing it in a calm that is truly your gift. Thank you.

Kathleen Hackett, the Zen woman, hipster, cookbook writer. You survived working with me in the kitchen—which is more than I can say for dozens of young chefs! You captured my voice, thoughts, and emotions in every word. Thank you.

Michael Psaltis, my agent. I'm sure you wanted to mute some of those long-winded conversations—but what a great book! Thank you.

Chefs Brian Gruskin, Steve Koustoumbaris, and Chris Marino. I know I'm crazy, but thanks for reminding me and helping me through all the recipes and mise en place. Thank you.

210   The Gianni, general manager extraordinaire, who really needs no introduction, for helping to organize the photo shoots and cleaning up the mess I left behind. Thank you.

Christopher Hirsheimer and Melissa Hamilton, renaissance women, artistic gurus, and photographic team recherché. Whoever said the second one is easier? You guys are genius! Thank you.

INDEX

ABOUT THE AUTHOR

Michael Psilakis is responsible for putting Modern Greek cuisine on the culinary map. He has earned many of the food world's highest honors, including a Michelin star and a James Beard Award nomination, and was named Chef of the Year by *Bon Appétit* and *Esquire*. His first book, *How to Roast a Lamb*, was published in 2009. He owns the restaurants Kefi, Fishtag, and MP Taverna in New York.